Becoming a Better Reader and Writer

WITHDRAWN

BOOKS MAY BE RENEWED
ONCE BY PHONE: 953-2253

DATE DUE

MAY 1 2 2003			
MAY 1 3 2003			
FEB 1 2 2013			
FEB 1 4 2013			

GAYLORD · PRINTED IN U.S.A.

Becoming a Better Reader and Writer

George Cuomo
University of Massachusetts, Amherst

Thomas Y. Crowell
Harper & Row, Publishers
New York, Hagerstown, San Francisco, London

Sponsoring Editor: Phillip Leininger
Project Editor: Rhonda Roth
Production Supervisor: Kewal K. Sharma
Compositor: Cherry Hill Composition
Printer and Binder: The Murray Printing Company
Art Studio: Danmark & Michaels Inc.

Becoming a Better Reader and Writer

Copyright © 1978 by Harper & Row, Publishers, Inc.

All rights reserved. Printed in the United States of America. No part of this book may be used or reproduced in any manner whatsoever without written permission except in the case of brief quotations embodied in critical articles and reviews. For information address Harper & Row, Publishers, Inc., 10 East 53rd Street, New York, N.Y. 10022.

Published simultaneously in Canada by Fitzhenry & Whiteside, Ltd., Toronto.

Library of Congress Cataloging in Publication Data

Cuomo, George.
   Becoming a better reader and writer.

  1. College readers. 2. English language—Rhetoric.
3. Reading I. Title.
PE1417.C78 1978   808'.042   77-17465
ISBN 0-690-00890-2

Acknowledgments

Grateful acknowledgment is made for use of the following material:

Mortimer J. Adler, from *How To Read A Book* (New York: Simon & Schuster). Copyright © 1940, 1967 by Mortimer J. Adler. Reprinted by permission of Simon & Schuster, a division of Gulf & Western Corporation.

George Barlow, "City Roses." Copyright © by George Barlow. Reprinted by permission of George Barlow.

Anthony Burgess, "Is America Falling Apart?" Copyright © 1971 by The New York Times Company. Reprinted by permission.

David L. Cohen, "Do American Men Like Women?" *Atlantic* (August 1946). Copyright © 1946, ® 1974 by The Atlantic Monthly Company, Boston, Mass. Reprinted by permission of the author and The Atlantic Monthly Company.

Michael S. Harper, "Savage." Copyright © by Michael S. Harper. Reprinted by permission of Michael S. Harper.

Bernard Malamud, "Idiots First." Reprinted by permission of Farrar, Straus & Giroux, Inc. from *Idiots First* by Bernard Malamud. Copyright © 1961, 1963 by Bernard Malamud.

Charles Simic, from *Dismantling the Silence* (New York: George Braziller, 1971). Reprinted by permission.

Robin Skelton, from "Comment" in *The Malahat Review*, no. 23 (July 1972).

William Stafford, "Judgments," from *The Rescued Year*. Copyright © 1966 by William E. Stafford. By permission of Harper & Row, Publishers, Inc.

Lynn White, Jr., "Educating Women in a Man's World," *Atlantic* (February 1950). Copyright © 1950 by The Atlantic Monthly Company, Boston, Mass. Reprinted by permission of the author and The Atlantic Monthly Company.

Charles E. Wyzanski, "Brandeis," *Atlantic* (November 1956). Copyright © 1956 by The Atlantic Monthly Company, Boston, Mass. Reprinted by permission of the author and The Atlantic Monthly Company.

W. B. Yeats, from "The Second Coming." Reprinted with permission of Macmillan Publishing Co., Inc. from *Collected Poems of William Butler Yeats*. Copyright 1924 by Macmillan Publishing Co., Inc., renewed 1952 by Bertha Georgie Yeats. Also reprinted by permission of M. B. Yeats, Miss Anne Yeats, and The Macmillan Co. of London & Basingstoke.

Contents

A Personal Note ix

A Reader's Checklist x

Chapter 1. Reading and Writing: A Long-Range View *1*

Chapter 2. Reading More Efficiently: Rate and Comprehension *3*

Chapter 3. Using Language More Effectively *13*

Chapter 4. A Basic Reading Pattern for Exposition: The Preliminary Survey *16*

Chapter 5. A Basic Reading Pattern for Exposition: Details and Difficulties *22*

Chapter 6. Writing Exposition *28*

Chapter 7. Evaluating What You Read: Persuasive Writing *37*

Chapter 8. Writing Persuasion *46*

Chapter 9. Reading Imaginative Literature: Stories, Novels, Plays, Poems *52*

Chapter 10. Writing about Literature *76*

Chapter 11. Remembering What You Read: Studying and Test Taking *83*

Chapter 12. Becoming a Regular Reader *90*

Suggested Readings *91*

A Personal Note

This book in one sense grew out of more than 20 years of college teaching, and everything in it has survived the test of classroom usefulness. But my interest in reading and writing goes beyond my commitment as a teacher. My own experience as a writer, I like to think, has produced a respect for the art and the craft that I am always delighted to see in others. And like all writers, I dream sometimes of a nation of good and enthusiastic readers, and have tried here to do my bit to help realize that tantalizing ideal.

George Cuomo

George Cuomo has combined the careers of teaching and writing. For over 20 years he has taught composition, creative writing, and literature in universities in the United States and Canada and is currently professor of English and a member of the MFA program in creative writing at the University of Massachusetts. He has worked as a newspaper reporter and copy editor, and as a technical, public relations, and advertising writer. His fiction, poetry, and essays have appeared widely in such magazines as *Saturday Review*, *The Nation*, and *Saturday Evening Post*, as well as in many literary quarterlies and anthologies. He was recently awarded a National Foundation of the Arts award for fiction. His publications include *Pieces from a Small Bomb*, *The Hero's Great Great Great Great Great Grandson*, *Among Thieves*, *Bright Day, Dark Runner*, *Jack Be Nimble*, "Sing Choir of Angels," and "Geronimo and the Girl Next Door."

A Reader's Checklist

When Reading Exposition

- Begin by quickly surveying for an overall view of an author's subject, main point, and organization
- Read rapidly and alertly
- Actively seek out meaning, emphasizing key words, phrases and ideas
- Adapt your approach to the demands of the material and your purpose in reading it
- Emphasize the most important and helpful parts of a work: the title, introduction, conclusion, beginnings and ends of paragraphs, transitions, and section headings
- Seek a clear understanding of main ideas
- Fit details into meaningful patterns
- Recapitulate in your mind what you have learned and what you want to retain

When Reading Persuasive Writing

- Distinguish carefully between fact and opinion, between a proof and an assertion
- Evaluate a writer's means of persuasion in terms of relevance, completeness, and logical consistency
- Test a writer's conclusions by examining his or her supporting evidence
- Watch for signs that a writer might be "slanting" his or her presentation unfairly

When Reading Imaginative Writing

- Work toward an understanding of what is happening, why it is happening, and what the broader significance may be
- Respond alertly to the use of implication, suggestion, and other means of indirect expression
- Actively seek to discover the author's central concerns
- Consider individual elements as part of a unified whole
- Use your knowledge of narrative structure and poetic form to seek a fuller understanding of the writer's methods, purpose, and achievement
- Remember that literary works deal with complex and elusive areas of human existence, and that the "meaning" of these works cannot always be reduced to simple formulations

Chapter 1

Reading and Writing: A Long-Range View

"Give me a student who can truly read and write," a teacher is supposed to have exclaimed in an enthusiastic moment, "and the sky's the limit for both of us."

But educators are expected to extol the virtues of what they teach. A more impressive testimonial comes from college graduates who wish they'd learned to read and write better in school, and from their supervisors and employers who fervently wish the same.

Some years ago the professional journal, *Chemical Engineering News*, polled its audience to see what kinds of articles would be most popular. The scientists and technicians voted for practical instruction in the skills of reading and writing, and the surprised editors responded with a long three-part article on the subject.

No matter what professional field you enter, you'll probably spend a good part of your work time reading and writing reports, letters, memoranda, advertisements, critiques, technical papers, trade magazines, and specialized books.

Beyond our professional and social responsibilities, we all share a desire to understand and respond more deeply to the unique qualities of our existence. Language can entertain, move, excite, enrage, and illuminate. The works of the great novelists and poets of the past and present may seem vastly different from a book on sailboating, a spoof of spy novels, or a real or ghosted autobiography of a movie queen. But they share something too They all offer a means to escape or transcend, in a frivolous or deeply felt way, the narrow limits of our daily lives.

For all its practical usefulness, perhaps the ultimate value of language lies in its unique role in both forming and expressing a part of us that defies description. As Peter Farb writes in his book, *Word Play*:

> Other animals besides man stand upright, have clever fingers and cunning brains, use tools. But man alone possesses the capacity to speak languages of such richness that linguists are still unable to describe them fully. Speech and man first appeared on the planet together, developed together, and when one disappears the other will also. Human speech is not merely some improved form of animal communication; it is a different category altogether that separates man, inhabiting the far side of an unbridgeable chasm, from the beasts.

Your use of language is not merely a classroom matter. And your development of this skill will have repercussions in your life far beyond the walls of any school.

This book will not necessarily make you an excellent reader and writer. But it can help you become a much better one.

Students are usually quite ready to admit that there's a lot to learn about writing. They're familiar with the work of professional authors whose skill confirms the fact that writing is a difficult and demanding craft.

Such is not the case with reading. There's no recognizable class of professionals with whom students can compare themselves. Everybody's a reader, and there are no obvious distinctions between struggling amateur and polished professional.

Most students do not realize how well or how poorly they read, since they're rarely called upon to exhibit their skill in public. Whether pursued out of necessity or pleasure, reading is normally performed in solitude. This sense of reading as private and personal also causes people to resist any attempt to evaluate or change the techniques they use.

Many students of course improve as readers under the pressure of college work. People who read a great deal tend to be better at it than those who don't. But practice helps only if you practice the right things and do not merely reinforce bad habits.

In truth, there is as much to be learned about reading as about writing, and the reading problems of college students are usually the direct result of their lack of knowledge about the subject.

With few exceptions, good readers are trained readers. Such training requires a certain amount of work and commitment, but it takes relatively little time and is comfortably within the reach of any serious student.

This book will help you understand the reading process and show you how to use this understanding to develop more effective reading habits. Thus you will learn how to:

1. Read more rapidly and efficiently than you now do
2. Understand better, even when reading more rapidly
3. Achieve full understanding whenever you desire it
4. Improve your vocabulary as part of a natural and continuing process
5. Develop a basic reading pattern for the most common types of writing:
   a. Informative writing
   b. Persuasive writing
   c. Imaginative writing—stories, novels, poems, plays
6. Study more effectively
7. Plan and carry out a useful and enjoyable long-range reading program

This book will also encourage you to take advantage of your improved reading ability to bring about a similar improvement in your writing. You will learn how to

1. Organize and convey information more effectively
2. Present persuasive arguments in support of your ideas
3. Write about imaginative literature—stories, novels, poems, plays—so as to convey both the qualities of the literary work and your own reactions to these qualities
4. Write examination answers that will clearly demonstrate your knowledge of a subject

Good reading and writing techniques are no academic cure-all, nor can they by themselves assure you of future professional success. What they can do, however, is allow you to make full use of the intelligence and aptitude you possess. By becoming a better reader and writer, you will almost inevitably become a better student.

You won't be required to spend long hours studying or drilling, but you will have to possess a desire to learn and a willingness to discard long-held misconceptions. Great improvement is readily attainable, but it cannot simply be handed to you. You have to reach out for it.

Chapter 2

Reading More Efficiently: Rate and Comprehension

HOW FAST DO YOU READ?

If like most people you read more slowly than you should, you'll learn in this chapter why this is so. You'll also learn how you can read twice as fast as you now do, without any loss in pleasure or understanding. In fact, by increasing your reading speed you will in all likelihood also increase both your enjoyment and your comprehension.

Learning to read more rapidly is an important first step in becoming a good reader. No one who always reads slowly—regardless of his reasons for doing so—can consider himself a skilled and efficient reader. A reasonable increase in your speed, therefore, serves as the initial step in your general program of reading improvement.

Before we explore the reasoning behind this statement, you will probably want to determine your own normal reading rate. It takes only a few minutes, and your performance will give you a better perspective on the discussion that follows.

Directions

Read the following passage at your *normal rate*. Read for understanding, in the same way you would read an article in your favorite magazine. Do not try to go either faster or slower than usual, for if you alter your normal reading habits, the results will be misleading.

Time yourself carefully. Note the exact time you begin and end, and determine how many minutes and seconds it takes you to read the passage. The table at the end of the selection will enable you to compute your reading rate in words per minute (WPM).

Start Timing Here

As far back as I can remember, there have been complaints about the schools for not teaching the young to write and speak well. The complaints have focused mainly on the products of high school and college. An elementary school diploma never was expected to certify great competence in these matters. But after four or eight more years in school, it seemed reasonable to hope for a disciplined ability to perform these basic acts. English courses were, and for the most part still are, a staple ingredient in the high school curriculum. Until recently, freshman English was a required course in every college. These courses were supposed to develop skill in writing the mother tongue. Though less emphasized than writing, the ability to speak clearly, if not with eloquence, was also supposed to be one of the ends in view.

The complaints came from all sources. Businessmen, who certainly did not expect too much, protested the incompetence of the youngsters who came their way after school. Newspaper editorials by the score echoed their protests and added a voice of their own, expressing the misery of the editor who had to blue-pencil the stuff college graduates passed across his desk.

Teachers of freshman English in college have had to do over again what should have been completed in high school. Teachers of other college courses have complained about the impossibly sloppy and incoherent English which students hand in on term papers and examinations.

And anyone who has taught in the graduate school or in a law school knows that a B.A. from our best colleges means very little with reference to a student's skill in writing or speaking. Many a candidate for the Ph.D. has to be coached in the writing of his dissertation, not from the point of view of scholarship or scientific merit but with respect to the minimum requirements of simple, clear, straightforward English. My colleagues in the law school frequently cannot tell whether a student does or does not know the law because of his inability to express himself coherently on a point in issue.

I have mentioned only writing and speaking, not reading. Until very recently, no one paid much attention to the even greater and more prevalent incompetence in reading, except, perhaps, the law professors who, ever since the introduction of the case method of studying law, have realized that half the time in a law school must be spent in teaching the student how to read cases. They thought, however, that this burden rested peculiarly on them, that there was something very special about reading cases. They did not realize that if college graduates had a decent skill in reading, the more specialized technique of reading cases could be acquired in much less than half the time now spent.

One reason for the comparative neglect of reading and the stress on writing and speaking is a point I have already mentioned. Writing and speaking are, for most people, so much more clearly *activities* than reading is. Since we associate skill with activity, it is a natural consequence of this error to attribute defects in writing and speaking to lack of technique, and to suppose that failure in reading must be due to moral defect—to lack of industry rather than of skill. The error is gradually being corrected. More and more attention is being paid to the problem of reading. I do not mean that the educators have yet discovered what to do about it, but they have finally realized that the schools are failing just as badly, if not worse, in the matter of reading, as in writing and speaking.

Mortimer J. Adler, *How To Read a Book*

Stop Timing Here

After determining the time it took you to read this selection (611 words), to the nearest fifteen seconds, find your reading rate in the accompanying table.

Reading Time	Rate in WPM
30 seconds	1222
45 seconds	815
1 minute	611
1 minute, 15 seconds	490
1 minute, 30 seconds	410
1 minute, 45 seconds	350
2 minutes	305
2 minutes, 15 seconds	270
2 minutes, 30 seconds	245
2 minutes, 45 seconds	220
3 minutes	205
3 minutes, 15 seconds	190
3 minutes, 30 seconds	175
3 minutes, 45 seconds	163
4 minutes	153
4 minutes, 15 seconds	144
4 minutes, 30 seconds	136
4 minutes, 45 seconds	128
5 minutes	122

This rate is not absolute, but rather a useful indication of your speed in reading simple, easily understood prose. You can now see (Figure 2-1) how well you did.

If you read 500 WPM or better, you can consider yourself a fast reader. Even you, however, can profit from learning to read still more efficiently. If your rate is average for a college freshman, 300 to 325 WPM, you read too slowly and should work for improvement. The average college freshman is not a rapid (nor a good) reader. If your rate is below 250 WPM, you are a very slow reader and would gain a great deal by learning to read more rapidly.

HOW FAST SHOULD YOU READ?

Suppose you and a classmate are given the same assignment. Assume that your rate is average for a college freshman—300 WPM—whereas your classmate's is 600. No matter how long the assignment is, your classmate will complete it in half the time it takes you. (He'll probably also understand and remember it better.)

Even wider variations are common among freshmen. Some read at 125 WPM, others at 900 WPM. Both figures represent exceptional cases, but a spread between 180 and 600 WPM is not unusual. Thus a one-hour reading assignment for some students takes others more than three times as long.

Later in this chapter you will learn how you can

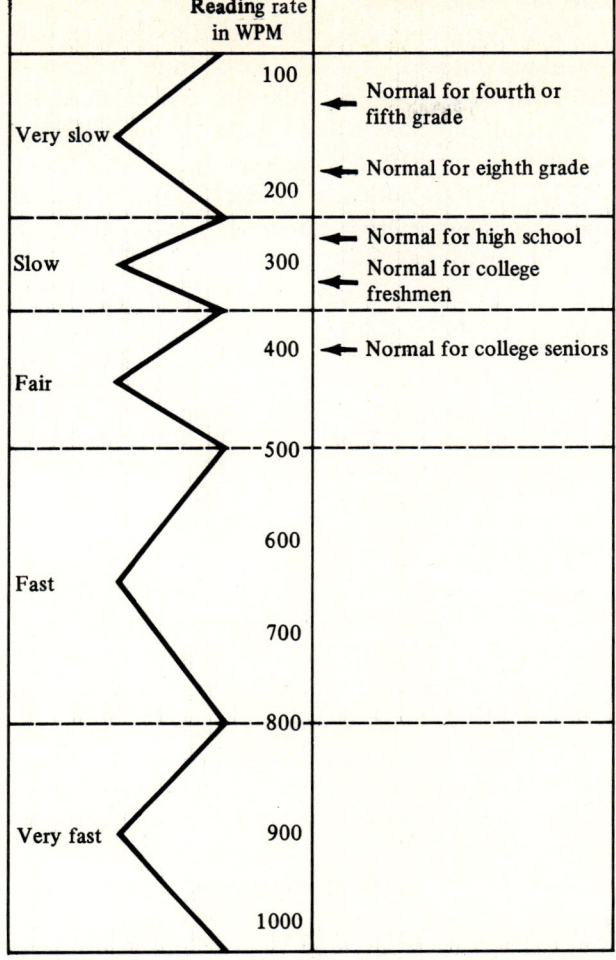

Figure 2-1

work as efficiently as your better trained classmates by doubling your present reading rate.

But, you say, *Will I be able to understand what I read?* Everyone can probably recall a teacher telling a class that a certain assignment had to be read "slowly and carefully." This is perhaps why so many students mistakenly believe that, in terms of reading effectiveness, "slowly" means the same as "carefully."

The most useful concept in discussing reading speed and comprehension is that of reading *efficiency*. Obviously, speed alone would be of little value if it were accompanied by a loss in comprehension. But it would be of great value if it could be achieved with *no* loss in comprehension.

As we will see, reasonable improvements in reading rate do not cause any loss in comprehension, because these increases result from the development of better reading skills. Thus a person who learns to read twice as fast as he does now, while maintaining his present ability to understand, will also read twice as efficiently.

But feelings about the whole matter of reading rates run high, and misconceptions are widespread. The nature of the reading process itself is frequently misunderstood or ignored. It's important, therefore, to examine some of these misconceptions before going on.

Unfortunately, the term "speed-reading" is often used as a means of labeling—and dismissing—the whole area of reading improvement. No one knows exactly what "speed-reading" means, yet it offers a convenient target for those who wish to discredit any reasonable attempt at reading improvement.

Extremists on both sides frequently manage to becloud the real issues. On the one hand, we see full-page newspaper advertisements assuring us that we can read 10,000, 15,000, or 20,000 WPM. On the other hand, extremists from the opposing side attack these inflated claims as typical of *all* reading improvement programs. Why not, asked one outraged critic, keep reading faster and faster until you can read all six volumes of Gibbon's *Decline and Fall of the Roman Empire* over a cup of instant coffee?

This is of course silly. Why not, one might suggest in turn, dutifully train ourselves to read slower and slower until it takes a full minute to read a single word? We could then spend something like 21,000 hours—or 2626 working days—moseying through *Decline and Fall*.

The point isn't whether a person should—or can—read 20,000 WPM. Reasonably enough, it should be agreed that unlimited speed is not a practical goal for the vast majority of people. At the same time it should also be admitted that there's no great virtue in excessive slowness.

The real issue is whether or not a person should simply *accept* the reading rate he happens to have as both inevitable and ideal. In other words, whether or not the average college student reading 300 WPM would be a lot better off if he could read effectively at 600 WPM, or perhaps even 800 or 1000 WPM.

The evidence is quite convincing that he would be better off. A rate of 300 WPM not only keeps a person from reading efficiently but often keeps him from reading at all. Faced with the prospect of having to spend six hours on an average book, he frequently decides he simply does not have the time. His real problem is that he has only two alternatives: six hours or no hours.

This brings us to an important and generally neglected point: A person does not have a *single* reading rate. He has—or should have—many rates. He should be able to read as rapidly or as slowly as he wants.

But all people have what can be considered a

base rate (the rate you tested yourself for a few pages back) at which they normally read more-or-less average material. It is from this base rate that they should speed up or slow down in accordance with the demands of the material and their purpose in reading it.

A person with a low base rate, however, rarely varies significantly. If he reads only 250 WPM, he can't go much faster because he's too unskilled and hampered by too many bad habits. And, given this base rate, he would hardly want to go much slower.

A reader operating from a base of 600 to 800 WPM has a far broader range of potential variation. The techniques he's learned that have enabled him to achieve this rate also allow him to move up easily to 1000 WPM for casual reading. And of course he can always slow down as much as he wants for studying or for reading difficult or technical material.

It's not the rapid reader who's a slave to speed. It's the slow reader who's a slave to slowness.

Perhaps the best way to discuss the most prevalent misconceptions is to consider them one at a time. It's important that you approach this discussion with an open mind and a willingness to reconsider some of your long-held beliefs.

Misconception: Fast readers are sloppy readers.

This results from the "slowly-and-carefully" fallacy mentioned earlier. Actually, the opposite is true. Fast readers are active, alert, and efficient. They look for main ideas, key points, and the elements of structure and organization that will help them grasp the writer's meaning.

Slow readers, however, tend to be aimless and unskilled. Their concentration is poor, and their thoughts wander. In part, this is because they are working too far below their capacity to stay alert and interested. In effect, they lie back passively and wait for understanding to come to them. All the work and responsibility, they feel, falls upon the writer.

To a large extent a fast reader gets more out of written material simply because he looks for more, and because he's learned how to look and what to look for.

Misconception: Only very bright people can read rapidly.

The truth is that any person of normal intelligence and good eyesight should be able to read and understand average material at a rate of 500 to 1000 WPM. Thousands of typical students have learned to do so. The goal is a perfectly realistic one.

Misconception: A rapid rate may work for light reading, but you can't read Shakespeare that way, or a sociology text, and you certainly can't study chemistry that way.

As we've mentioned, even poor readers tend to speed up or slow down slightly from their base rates, according to the difficulty of the material. The significant fact is that a faster reader can vary more freely, and from a much better starting point.

The way fast and slow readers might alter their speeds under different circumstances is shown in the accompanying table.

	Slow	Fast
Normal base rate	300	600
Rate for easy material	400	800
Rate for difficult material	200	400
Rate for intensive study	150	300

These are of course only projected figures, but they reflect typical patterns. Anyone with a base rate twice as high as another person's can probably read *everything* approximately twice as fast, and with just as much, or more, comprehension.

This does *not* mean, as the table shows, that a person with a rapid rate has to read everything at his top speed. A skilled reader can be compared to an automobile with several forward speeds, each appropriate for a different situation. Francis Bacon showed over 300 years ago that intelligent readers knew about shifting rates long before mechanics knew about shifting gears: "Some books are to be tasted, others to be swallowed, and some few to be chewed and digested."

Misconception: If you read rapidly, you have no time to look up words, to reflect, or to reread difficult passages.

There's no reason for this to be so. A fast reader can stop as often as a slow one to look up words or ruminate upon the material. He will still finish sooner and will understand and remember as much or more. And whenever he wishes, he can of course go back and read something again. It should be pointed out, however, that a fast reader has a much better chance of understanding the first time around.

Misconception: Fast readers are always rushing. They can never relax and enjoy themselves.

A fast reader working at his base rate is not rushing any more than a slow reader going along at *his* base rate. Again, it has to be understood that superior speed is the result of skill, training, and alertness—not of hurrying.

Misconception: Even if rapid reading is legitimate and valuable, it can be achieved only through long years of study and practice.

It's true that most fast readers have read a good deal, and most slow readers have not. But even widely experienced readers are sometimes very slow because certain bad habits, of which they're probably unaware, have held them back.

No one is born knowing how to read; everyone must be taught, and they can be taught well or poorly. Ironically, the strongest opposition to the teaching of effective reading techniques comes from those who base their arguments on "literary" considerations. Yet these are often the same people who complain that schools don't spend enough time teaching students how to *write* well. Give them more spelling, they demand, more punctuation, grammar, sentence structure, and paragraph development. A knowledge of fundamental writing techniques thus seems highly desirable, but any attempt to teach comparable reading techniques is considered somehow an affront to all lovers of literature. If training and knowledge are desirable in one discipline, might they not also help in the other?

Obviously, you can't significantly improve your reading rate overnight. But if you're an average reader, you *can* double your present rate, without any loss in comprehension, in 30 days by working at it a few minutes every day. You can do this by eliminating whatever bad habits you have and by improving your basic attitudes and techniques.

HOW YOU READ

The ultimate purpose of reading of course is intellectual, emotional, or psychological. But the stimulators of this mental activity—the words and thoughts of the author—are transmitted to the brain by a physical process. Thus, for all its ethereal possibilities, reading is also a learned muscular activity in which certain skills are employed, either more or less successfully.

The Movement of the Eyes

Like most people, you probably assume that your eyes travel across a page in a smooth, continuous movement. Actually, the eyes move jerkily. In covering a line of type, they make several abrupt stops of short duration.

It is only during these stops that the actual reading is done. The eye does not see while it is moving. The impression that you can see while the eye is in motion results from the same effect that makes a series of still photographs, projected at sixteen frames per second, seem to be a motion picture. Your brain retains an image for a brief period, and thus you're not aware of the blank spaces in between. But in reading, as at all other times, your eyes must come to a stop, even though very briefly, in order to send an image to the brain.

Through the use of special cameras, it has been shown that fast readers make fewer stops per line than slow readers. Since each stop takes time, the more stops you make, the slower you read. This simple difference is crucial to the role of physical activity in determining reading speed and efficiency.

Fast readers make fewer stops because they see more during each one. They make use of their *peripheral vision* to see not only what lies at the focus of their vision, but also what is on the edges, or periphery.

Studies of eye movements during reading indicate that most readers see somewhere between 1.3 and 2.6 words per fixation. It's also been determined that even fast readers are normally limited to approximately four fixations per second. Assuming that the subjects are actually reading and not merely skimming, we can project from these figures an indication of the significance of eye movements in reading rates.

At 4 fixations a second, a reader makes 240 fixations per minute. If he sees 1.3 words per stop, his rate will be approximately 320 words per minute. If he is able to see 2.6 words per stop, his rate will be 640 WPM. These are of course only typical figures, but they indicate a basic reason for the wide variation in reading speeds among typical college students.

It should be pointed out that reading *stamina* is also influenced by the frequency of fixations. Because slow readers do a lot more starting and stopping, they have to work longer and harder than fast readers to cover the same amount of material.

Finding Key Words

In addition to taking advantage of their peripheral vision, fast readers have learned to concentrate on key words. For instance, a very slow reader reads every word in the following sentence:

The boy went over to the corner of the room and sat on the chair that he happened to find there.

A fast reader, however, probably concentrates on the italicized words:

The *boy* *went* over to the *corner* of the *room* and *sat* on the *chair* that he happened to find *there*.

And of these, he may respond primarily to only three: "boy," "corner," and "chair." He sees all the words because he can take in whole phrases with a single fixation, but he emphasizes the most important ones and thus quickly and efficiently grasps the meaning of the sentence.

Finding Thought Patterns

The basic unit of verbal communication is not the word. It is the thought. A newspaper editor once said that in poor writing "words take the place of ideas." The same thing occurs in poor reading. A slower reader is overly concerned with the means of communication—the words—and insufficiently aware of what is actually being communicated—the thoughts.

A slow reader, for instance, would read the following sentence word by word:

> At the conclusion of the festivities the general and his aides departed from the ancient manor house and rode all night to rejoin the troops in the field.

Yet the sentence breaks naturally into thought groups (as do almost all sentences) and should be read with proper emphasis on these groups and the key words within them:

> (At the *conclusion* of the *festivities*) (the *general* and his *aides*) (*departed* from the *ancient manor house*) (and *rode all night*) (to *rejoin* the *troops* in the *field*.)

ELIMINATING YOUR BAD HABITS

Most bad habits are holdovers from early reading experiences at home or at school. All of them are easy to recognize once you learn about them. They are also, as you will see, relatively easy to eliminate.

Lipreading

If you form the words you read by moving your lips, you are a lip-reader. All lip-readers are slow readers. Lip movement limits your reading rate to the rate at which you speak, since it takes just as long to form the words with the lips as it would to say them aloud. Even a very rapid talker can speak only about 300 WPM, and most people speak only about 200 WPM. As long as a person moves his lips, his reading will be restricted to this very slow rate.

You can discover if you're a lip-reader by placing your finger lightly on your lips while you are reading. If you lip-read, you will be able to feel slight movements.

Throat Vocalization

Throat vocalization occurs when the vocal cords are partially activated during reading, as if to sound the words while not actually doing so. Although far more common than lipreading, this is less obvious and therefore usually goes unnoticed. It's harmful because, like lipreading, it holds your reading down to the much slower pace of speech.

To find out if you vocalize, place your thumb and forefinger lightly at the sides of your throat, just behind the thyroid cartilage (the male Adam's apple). If you vocalize, you will feel a series of faint movements in the vocal cords as you read.

Auditory Reading

An auditory reader "hears" the words as he reads them, as if an inner voice were reciting them aloud in his head. This is by far the most common deterrent to rapid reading, for almost every untrained reader is an auditory reader. Like the first two habits, it probably results from the fact that most children learn to read by reading aloud. Again, like the other faults, auditory reading limits your reading speed to the very slow rate of speech.

Normally you should hear nothing when you read, and this is true of a good reader. In this instance, however, there are exceptions which ought to be noted, such as in the reading of poetry or drama, or any piece of writing in which the sounds are important. Such material is ideally read aloud, to allow the sound patterns to function as they were intended to by the author. Since this isn't always feasible, auditory reading is the next best thing for these works, as it lets the reader "hear" the words in his mind. A good reader of course can produce an auditory response whenever he wishes. In most reading, however, impulses to the brain are transmitted most efficiently by visual, not auditory, means.

Regression

The habit of *automatically* going back to reread a word or phrase is called *regression*. It should be emphasized that this is an unconscious habit, something the reader is often unaware of, and that it is done *without regard to the difficulty of the material*. People who are regressive readers have developed a forward-backward pattern as a standard part of their eye movements in reading, and follow it as slavishly as a beginner follows the steps of a new dance.

A typical regressive reader, for instance, consistently reads with perhaps three or four forward movements and then one backward movement. And he does this with everything, from a comic strip to a biology text.

Regressive reading, therefore, should not be confused with an occasional *decision* to go back and reread difficult, notable, or poorly written material. This is a conscious act, undertaken for specific reasons.

Regressive reading is *not* a matter of choice; it is unconscious, automatic, and unvarying. It is harmful because it generally weakens, not strengthens, comprehension, and because it significantly slows down a person's reading rate.

Most material can be easily understood the first time. If you have trouble understanding something, you can of course go back and reread whenever you wish. But you should not fall into the rigid forward-backward pattern of a true regressive reader. The roots of this habit can probably be found in a reader's lack of confidence in his ability to understand. He keeps going back to reassure himself that he hasn't missed anything. Unfortunately, a regressive reader usually *does* have poor comprehension, but his difficulties are only magnified by the hesitant and disrupted progress his regression produces.

In general, all these habits should be avoided. Recent studies have shown, however, that everyone activates the speech organs to a slight extent while reading. These faint traces of the speech process are negligible. You should be concerned only with residual speech movements or regressive habits that are prominent enough to interfere with the effectiveness of your reading.

If you wish, you can work separately to eliminate any of these habits. Lipreading, for instance, can be cured by reading for a time with your lips consciously pressed together. You can eliminate throat vocalization by reading for a period with your fingers lightly at your throat, at the same time consciously suppressing any movement of the vocal apparatus. Similarly, you can also make a conscious effort to quiet the voice in your head and keep your eyes moving forward without regression. It's much more effective, however, to eliminate these bad habits as part of a single comprehensive program of reading improvement, such as the one we now set forth.

DOUBLING YOUR READING RATE IN THIRTY DAYS

We will now show how you can increase your reading speed by

1. Making fewer stops per line
2. Reading more during each stop
3. Concentrating on key words
4. Breaking sentences into logical thought groups
5. Eliminating bad reading habits

Since reading is a composite skill, you should learn to do all these things in proper synchronization. The best approach is therefore one that treats reading as a unified phenomenon, not as a collection of separate techniques.

Some colleges have reading laboratories equipped with devices to help students increase their speed and comprehension. Such devices, though, are expensive and not always available, and you can obtain the same results working alone without mechanical aids. In fact, there's an advantage to using the printed page, since students who've increased their reading rates with the aid of machines sometimes have problems transferring the increase to book or magazine reading. In this program, you will work directly with a book of your own choice. There'll be no expense, nor any need for special equipment or facilities.

Simply stated, this is what you are to do:

For the next 30 days, read as fast as you possibly can for a few minutes every day.

A great many teachers, including the author, have guided numerous students through this program. Some students began with rates under 200 WPM, others at better than 500 WPM. Regardless of their speed at the beginning, they almost invariably could read twice as fast at the end, with equal or better understanding. The program is neither complicated nor difficult. But you have to understand and follows the directions, and you have to perform your task faithfully every day for the next 30 days.

Thirty-Day Reading Program

Directions

1. Select a full-length book, preferably nonfiction, that is relatively straightforward in style and subject matter.
2. Use the chart in Figure 2-2 to keep a daily record of your progress.
3. If you have not already done so, test yourself for bad reading habits as explained in the preceding section. List any that you have at the top of the chart.
4. Determine your normal reading rate for the book you have chosen. Timing yourself carefully, read for two minutes in the book and count the exact number of words. Since you have read for two minutes, divide the number of words by two to find your normal reading rate in WPM. Do *not* read rapidly for this test. Read for comprehension, at your normal, unhurried rate. Enter the result in the space on the chart labeled "normal rate at beginning."
5. Every day for thirty days read your book *as fast as you possibly can without worrying at the moment about comprehension.* Each day enter on the chart the number of minutes you have read at this extremely fast rate, the ap-

CHART FOR THIRTY-DAY
RAPID-READING PROGRAM

Bad Habits:

Normal Rate at Beginning	WPM
Normal Rate at End	WPM
Increase in WPM	WPM

Day	Date	Minutes Spent Reading	Number of Words Read at Forced Rate	Forced Rate in WPM
1				
2				
3				
4				
5				
6				
7				
8				
9				
10				
11				
12				
13				
14				
15				
16				
17				
18				
19				
20				
21				
22				
23				
24				
25				
26				
27				
28				
29				
30				

Figure 2-2

proximate number of words you have read, and the rate you have obtained in WPM.

These daily computations need not be exact, as they serve only as a rough check on your progress. Since a nonfiction book usually has few uneven lines of dialogue, you can easily simplify your calculations. First, count the words on several pages and determine the average for a single page. You can then use this average figure to compute your rate each day:

$$\frac{\text{Pages read} \times \text{Average no. of words per page}}{\text{Minutes required}}$$

$$= \text{rate in WPM}$$

If on a given day you read 8 pages in 5 minutes and your book averages 400 words per page, you can compute your rate in this way:

$$\frac{8 \times 400}{5} = \frac{3200}{5} = 640 \text{ WPM}$$

This naturally is not your normal rate. You have achieved it artificially by forcing yourself to read at a greatly accelerated speed. You will read at this forced rate only during the few minutes you spend on the program each day. It serves merely as a training device and isn't intended to become a permanent part of your reading method.

6. Reading at this forced rate will be quite tiring, especially at first. Since forced reading is strenuous, plan to read for only three minutes a day for the first few days. When you can maintain a forced rate for three minutes without strain, lengthen your reading period to five minutes. Subsequent increases to eight, ten, fifteen, and perhaps twenty minutes should follow at fairly regular intervals, usually of about five days. By the end of the program you should be able to maintain a forced rate for fifteen or twenty minutes without great fatigue.

7. You should work every day at approximately the same time and under the same conditions. Don't try to read at a forced rate when you're tired or sleepy, and keep yourself free from distractions.

8. Consciously attempt to eliminate your bad reading habits as you progress through the daily exercises. If, for instance, you are a regressive reader, force yourself to read without going back.

9. After thirty days, again test yourself to determine your normal *unhurried* rate for the material in your book, just as you did in Step 4. Enter your new rate in the appropriate space at the top of the chart. Even though you do *not* seem to be rushing anymore, you should be reading approximately twice as fast as you were at the beginning, and with at least as much comprehension.

10. Test yourself again for bad reading habits. You should have eliminated any you had.

During the program, you may do as much other reading as you wish without any conscious alteration of your normal habits. You will probably discover, though, that you are already becoming a more discriminating reader, that you are looking for key words and main ideas and reading everything more alertly.

As you can see, this method is neither difficult nor time-consuming. In fact, some people distrust it because it sounds too easy. But it works. If you follow directions, you should have no difficulty doubling your normal reading rate.

Despite the simplicity of the method, there are some points you should bear in mind:

You must read as fast as you possibly can. The success of this method depends upon the maintenance of a *forced speed* during the exercise periods. Do not let yourself relax or slow down. Keep moving your eyes across the page as rapidly as you can. If you are reading at a truly forced rate, you will, especially at the beginning, feel the strain.

At the beginning, you will probably understand very little of what you read. Don't worry. Most people find that comprehension picks up considerably about the fifteenth day. By the end of the program your comprehension will have moved back toward normal, even though you're still reading at a forced rate. Do not, however, expect full comprehension while reading at this greatly accelerated rate. Concentrate on key words and main ideas.

Your forced rate should continue to increase throughout the program. At the beginning, aim for a forced rate that's about twice your normal rate. It will probably level off from time to time, then spurt ahead, and then level off again. It may even drop back occasionally, especially when you lengthen your daily reading period. But your forced rate should not level off for more than a few days at a time. Keep increasing your rate, even though you still do not understand much of what you are reading.

Most people are bothered by their initial inability to comprehend while reading at a forced rate. You should not, however, slow down in order to understand more. Force yourself to read as alertly as possible in order to understand at the more rapid rate.

If you begin, for instance, with a normal rate of 250 WPM, you should start with a forced rate of about 500 WPM. You will probably understand very little at this rate. Nonetheless you should gradually increase it—along with the number of minutes you spend reading each day—at fairly regular intervals throughout the thirty days. These increases should enable you to end up reading at a final forced rate of approximately 1000 WPM for fifteen minutes or more.

About the middle of the thirty-day period you will begin to note a gradual increase in your comprehension, even at this forced rate. By the end you'll have worked up to fairly good, but still partial, understanding while reading at the forced rate of 1000 WPM. When you resume your normal way of reading, you should easily be able to maintain a speed of 500 WPM—twice what you started with. And after training yourself to achieve partial understanding at 1000 WPM, you'll have no trouble maintaining your normal comprehension at 500 WPM.

It's not necessary to complete the thirty-day program before proceeding to the other chapters of this book. You should, however, begin the program immediately and plan to carry it through to its conclusion. Don't despair or give up along the way. If you stick with it, you'll achieve something of real value.

Maintaining Your Speed

After you've experienced the advantages of a more rapid, and more efficient, reading rate, it's unlikely that you'll fall back into the habit of slow, passive, or inattentive reading. But if you're concerned about this, check your base rate occasionally to make sure that it's satisfactory. Any losses that may have occurred can be easily made up by reading slightly faster than usual for a few days.

Extending the Program

You may wish to continue the program beyond thirty days, especially if your former base rate was so low that doubling still leaves it unsatisfactory. You should realize, though, that the most dramatic gains generally occur at the beginning of the program.

A person who increases his normal rate from 250 to 500 WPM during the first thirty days might expect, in another thirty days, to move up to 700 or 800 WPM. This is a substantial increase of course, but proportionately not as great as that achieved in the first thirty days.

Learning to read more rapidly should help you become a better reader in every way. This is true because you'll have increased your speed through greater alertness, greater skill in seeking out key words and logical groupings, and more effective concentration on the basic element of all writing—the thoughts the writing is intended to convey.

In other words, you'll have maintained, and possibly increased, your present comprehension while significantly improving your rate. This makes you not simply a faster reader, but a more efficient one.

Some Studies of the Reading Process

A great many experimental studies of the reading process have been carried out. The following sources, most of which offer extensive bibliographies, are of particular interest:

Anderson, Irving H. "Studies in the Eye Movements of Good and Poor Readers." *Psychological Monographs*, 48 (1937), 1–35. (One of the earliest studies of the physical aspects of reading.)

Berger, Allen. "Effectiveness of Four Methods of Increasing Reading Rate, Comprehension, and Flexibility—A Summary." *College and Adult Reading*, 5th Yearbook of the North Central Reading Association, 1968.

―――. "Flexibility and Speed in Reading." *Reading for All*, 4th International Reading Association World Congress on Reading, 1972. (A good summary of research in the field.)

Hafner, Lawrence E. "Improving Grade Point Averages through Reading-Study Skills Instruction." *New Frontiers in College and Adult Reading*, 15th Yearbook of the National Reading Conference, 1966.

Laycock, Frank. "Significant Characteristics of College Students with Varying Flexibility in Reading Rate: I. Eye Movements in Reading Prose." *Journal of Experimental Education*, 23 (1955), 311–19.

Nache, Phillip L. "Issues in the Speed Reading Controversy." *College Reading: Problems and Programs of Junior and Senior Colleges*, 21st Yearbook of the National Reading Conference, Vol. II, 1972.

Schale, Florence. "Measuring Degree and Rate of Visual Awareness during Growth in Rapid Reading on Television." *College Reading: Problems and Programs of Junior and Senior Colleges*, 21st Yearbook of the National Reading Conference, Vol. II, 1972.

Schmidt, Bernard. "The Purdue Developmental Reading Program—Progress and Problems." *College and Adult Reading*, 7th Yearbook of the North Central Reading Association, 1974.

Van Gilder, Lester L. "Speed Reading vs. Effective Developmental Reading." *College and Adult Reading*, 2nd Yearbook of the North Central Reading Association, 1963.

Walker, Robert Y. "A Qualitative Study of the Eye Movements of Good Readers," *American Journal of Psychology*, 51 (1938), 472–81. (One of the early influential studies in the field.)

Chapter 3

Using Language More Effectively

Assuming you've never seen the word before, can you figure out the meaning of "jargon" from its use in the following passage?

> That the discoveries made by men of science . . . should be made as widely known as possible would be, one might expect, their especial desire. And how else can this be done, if not by translating their thought from the technical jargon in which it is apt to be expressed into plain English which the world can understand?
>
> W. T. Stace, *The Snobbishness of the Learned*

The fact that you probably can illustrates the method by which you have learned most of the words you know: by observing them being used. An intelligent reader makes reasonable assumptions based on the context in which a word appears. He also looks for explanations or implied definitions which might accompany it, since writers often try to help readers understand difficult words.

(For example, you should now be able to develop a satisfactory definition of "context" from the preceding paragraph.)

The average college student is reputed to have a vocabulary of between 10,000 and 20,000 words. The vast majority of these were not learned from a dictionary. From childhood on, new words are acquired gradually and naturally by listening, speaking, reading, and writing. The more times you meet a word, the more exact your understanding of it becomes. Because this process takes place largely outside the classroom, people often underrate it. It nonetheless offers the best chance of long-range vocabulary improvement.

Although students frequently say, "I'm not a good reader (or writer) because I don't have a good vocabulary," the reverse is more often true. With few exceptions, a person's vocabulary is only as extensive as it has to be. People generally have poor vocabularies because their limited experience as readers and writers hasn't given them the opportunity to learn many words.

Nor should you assume that a poor vocabulary results from the failure to look up unfamiliar words immediately. Used intelligently, a dictionary can become the most valuable book you own, but that doesn't mean that you have to refer to it every time you come across an unfamiliar word.

THE NATURAL WAY TO IMPROVE YOUR VOCABULARY

Since a rich and useful vocabulary results from the *need* for such a vocabulary, the obvious advice is to read more. It is especially helpful to read in diverse fields, for each area of knowledge has its own specialized words. Regular reading of a good daily newspaper and a few serious magazines will introduce you to many more words than you would meet in conversation. The same is true for books. As simple as it sounds, you can best improve your command of the language by becoming a more enthusiastic reader than you are now. (See Chapter 12 for some suggestions about beginning a regular reading program.) Any reading you do will increase your effective vocabulary, even if you make no conscious effort to learn new words. But you can enhance this process by becoming more actively involved in it.

Although vocabulary improvement is often thought of as merely learning new words, there are really three ways in which a person can increase his vocabulary:

1. By learning new words
2. By learning new definitions of familiar words
3. By gaining a more precise understanding of a word's shadings and overtones

For example, after meeting it several times in various contexts, your understanding of the word "gadfly" might develop as follows.

Learning a new word. You would discover, either from the context or from the use of a dictionary, that "gadfly" usually refers to someone who annoys or irritates others.

Learning additional meanings. Upon seeing it used in a more literal sense, you'd learn that it also denotes any of a variety of flies that bite or annoy domestic animals and cattle. Referring to a dictionary, you'd discover that this is the older of the two meanings. The human's actions, therefore, were characterized because of their similarity to the insect's.

Gaining a more precise understanding. Through seeing it used in various instances, you'd probably conclude that today it usually refers to someone who thrives on criticizing others. A gadfly's criticisms, however, tend to be superficial. He "annoys and irritates" others but rarely wounds them very deeply.

You might then learn that the effect of the insect is similar to that of a gad, which is a pointed stick, or goad, used to drive cattle by pricking them sharply without injuring them.

Thus you would not call someone a gadfly who, after long study, suggests a restructuring of the American public education system. The term is obviously more appropriate for someone who persistently interrupts a club meeting with objections over procedure. Your "feeling" for the word would probably also suggest that it usually possesses a somewhat positive implication. A gadfly, in other words, is often viewed as an energetic, determined "little guy" whose harassing tactics keep the "big shots" on their toes.

When Should You Use a Dictionary?

What should you do, though, when you come across a word whose meaning cannot be determined from its context? Most students dutifully give the "proper" answer. You should, they insist, immediately look it up in a dictionary. Perhaps so, but few students do. Few teachers, writers, or scholars do either. An intelligent person should be able to use a dictionary as much or as little as he wishes. He shouldn't feel obligated to refer to it so often that it turns his reading into a distasteful chore.

The following guidelines suggest a realistic pattern of dictionary use. In general you should probably look up

1. *Words needed for comprehension or enjoyment.* If you can't figure out the meaning of a word from its context, yet need it to understand the passage, you should consult a dictionary. This is particularly true when you're reading a textbook, studying, or reading something in which you have a particular interest.
2. *Words you've met before but still do not understand.* Vocabulary growth should reflect your interests and needs. If you've met certain words before, there's a good chance you will again. They would therefore make a useful addition to your vocabulary.
3. *Words that you've met in your reading and wish to use in your writing.* You can't be a good reader if you're inattentive to the meanings of words, but it's nonetheless true that you don't need to know the *precise* definition of every word you come across. Most people would find the following sentence understandable even if they didn't know the exact meaning of "clique":

A small clique of army officers banded together at that time to oppose the new regulations.

What is called the *denotative* meaning of a word —its specific or objective equivalent, without reference to its tone or suggestion—is relatively easy to figure out. A clique, obviously, is a group formed around some common interest or agreement. But you wouldn't be able to learn from this sentence the usual *connotative* meaning of the word, which deals with its overtones and emotional content. If you wanted to use the word in an essay, however, you'd need to realize that "clique" almost always has an unfavorable connotation, as illustrated by the discussion of the word and its synonyms in Funk and Wagnall's *Standard College Dictionary*:

> *Clique, coterie, circle* and *set* denote a group of persons having a common interest. *Clique* suggests that this interest is selfish or hostile to a larger group, whereas *coterie* suggests amiable congeniality. A *circle* centers upon a person or an activity, and may be small or large: a sewing *circle*, scientific *circles*. *Set* suggests a large and loosely bound group: the fashionable *set*.

An awareness of these distinctions is indispensable when you write. Thus a dictionary should be used regularly whenever you wish, in effect, to move a word from your reading to your writing vocabulary.

Good readers and writers invariably possess an effective vocabulary, and any improvement in your use of language will benefit your reading and writing. But sheer size of vocabulary is not the primary consideration. Your goal should be to learn new words as they become useful to you and to use all words with care and accuracy.

Your language, after all, is an integral part of the way you view and respond to the world and is intimately bound up with your preceptions, consciousness, and sensitivity. George Orwell makes the point well in his essay, "Politics and the English Language":

> A man may take to drink because he feels himself to be a failure, and then fail all the more completely because he drinks. It is rather the same thing that is happening to the English Language. It becomes ugly and inaccurate because our thoughts are foolish, but the slovenliness of our language makes it easier for us to have foolish thoughts.

Perhaps the most important reason to devote some attention to your vocabulary is that your command of the language, as Orwell suggests, is irrevocably involved with your thought processes. Clarity and accuracy in the use of words strengthens not only the expression of your thoughts but the thinking of them too.

Chapter 4

A Basic Reading Pattern for Exposition: The Preliminary Survey

A writer usually undertakes one of three tasks:

1. To *inform* the reader (expository writing)
2. To *persuade* the reader to accept certain attitudes or conclusions (persuasive writing)
3. To *share* with the reader his thoughts, emotions, or experiences (imaginative writing: stories, novels, plays, poems)

Naturally, most writers have mixed purposes. Read, for instance, the following passage.

The principal charges brought against books are two. The first is the psychologist's assertion that all imaginative literature, fiction or verse, indulges daydreaming and makes it difficult for its devotees to adjust to the demands of reality. There is a small grain of sense in this position, but only a small one. Let us, however, swallow it whole; it still betrays a false identification of human weakness with a particular means of indulging it; like all puritanical reformers, the ascetic preacher of the Reality Principle argues that, if the means of indulgence are cut off, the desire will wither away, a doubtful proposition. I often spend time reading detective stories when I ought to be answering letters, but, if all detective stories were suppressed, I see no reason to believe that I should not find some other device for evading my duty.

The second, and more serious, objection to the printed word is that the language, sensibility and wisdom of literate persons are, in so many cases, inferior to that of the illiterate—the D. H. Lawrence pro-peasant position. How much substance is there in this? It is nonsense to talk of the "secondhand" experience gained from books in contrast to the "firsthand" experience gained from the bookless life, for human beings are not born, like the insects, fully equipped for life, but have to learn almost everything secondhand from others. If we were limited to our firsthand, that is, our sensory experience, we should still be living in trees on a diet of raw vegetables. If a literate person seems inferior to an illiterate, this means that the quality of experience he is gaining from his reading is inferior to that which a peasant gains from talking to his father or his neighbors. The remedy is not to stop him from reading but to persuade him to read better books.

W. H. Auden, *The World That Books Have Made*

Clearly this author has more than one purpose. He wants to *inform* the reader of the two "principal charges brought against books." He also hopes to *persuade* the reader to accept his rejection of these charges. Finally, he tries, at least indirectly, to *share* with the reader his thoughts, emotions, and experiences concerning the value of good books.

We will now set forth a basic reading pattern which can be varied for use in any reading situation, as well as for material of any length or difficulty. You can use it to skim (with good general comprehension) through a newspaper story, to study a textbook in detail, or to do anything in between. The way you use it will depend on your purpose in reading and on the kind of material being read.

In this chapter and the next we will describe the pattern in detail as it would be used on the most straightforward kind of material: pure exposition. In its pure state, exposition has only one purpose, and that is to inform. The author does not try to persuade the reader, nor to share feelings with him. For the time being, we can assume that all exposition is pure, uncontaminated by any purpose other than that of informing. (In reality of course such purity of type is unusual.)

In Chapter 7 we will show how your basic reading pattern should be varied and expanded in reading *persuasive* writing. And in Chapter 9 we will discuss additional techniques designed to help you read *imaginative literature*.

A BASIC READING PATTERN

The chances are that you read the way most people do. You find the first sentence on the first page and begin. This is probably true whether you've picked up an entertaining or informative magazine article, a detective story, a serious and complex novel, an economics text, a political tract, a set of carpentry directions, or your class notes from a literature course. You do what you've done all your life: You start at the beginning and stop at the end. What you are asked to consider now is the possibility that this approach—when followed for all your reading—is less than ideal.

For much of your reading, especially that pursued for pleasure and relaxation, this straightforward approach is perfectly natural. It can serve quite well for a person who can read rapidly and vary his speed when he wants to.

Yet this beginning-to-end method is not the only one, nor the most efficient. A good reader adjusts not only his speed to the situation, but his whole approach.

What we present here is a basic reading pattern that *can* be used for any kind of reading and *should* be used for important or demanding material. The choice of course is always yours. The value of this method is that it allows you, whenever you choose, to read, understand, and remember at your maximum potential. You won't always want to master material this thoroughly. As a good reader, though, you should be able to do so whenever you desire.

The basic reading pattern is composed of three steps:

1. (a) Making a preliminary survey, (b) recapitulation
2. (a) Filling in details, (b) recapitulation
3. (a) Clearing up difficulties, (b) recapitulation

This approach is based on certain principles of effective reading:

A reader should work from the general to the particular. It's hard to grasp details without knowing the overall pattern of which they're a part. Possibly the most serious reading weakness of college students is their tendency to read without a focus, without a central idea to which they can relate details. The basic reading pattern requires the reader to begin by seeking out the unifying focus of a work as a whole.

Several rapid readings are better than a single slow one. Given a certain amount of time, it's more efficient to spend it on two or more fast readings than one slow reading. Because of the speed at which they are performed, these additional readings will not take any extra time.

Purposeful reading is superior to aimless reading. This is the same principle we've stated before: An active and alert reader functions far better than an aimless, passive one. As much as possible, you should have specific goals, questions you want answered, and points you are looking for. The basic reading pattern encourages this by setting forth clearly defined objectives for each of the three steps.

For purposes of simplification, we introduce the pattern as it would be used on article-length—or chapter-length—material. We'll then show how it can be easily modified for full-length books.

Step 1a: Making a Preliminary Survey

The purpose of a preliminary survey is to gain a rapid overall view of the author's major concerns by determining his

1. Subject
2. Organization
3. Main point

The author's *subject* is simply what he is writing about. This is the first thing you should look for, and you should try to phrase it as specifically as possible. "Education" could be the subject of a magazine piece, but it's so broadly stated that it could apply to innumerable articles. "Test score results" is more exact and therefore more helpful. "A comparison of math scores in various school systems" is still better.

Practice will quickly increase your skill in finding and phrasing an author's subject in precise terms. Once you form the habit of looking for the subject of an article and stating it succinctly, you'll see how easy it is, and how helpful.

The author's *organization* can be defined as his pattern and sequence of presentation. In discussing high school math scores an author may compare nationwide test results for a typical large school and a typical small one—or for representative groups of large and small schools, urban and rural schools, or private and public schools. He may study the relationship, if any, of test scores to certain economic or social conditions, average class size, faculty quality, or any number of other factors. He may interview students, teachers or administrators from different schools. If the article is based on a long-range study, he may discuss the relationship of high school test scores with students' future success in college math courses.

A great many approaches are possible for almost any subject. Once you've determined the author's subject, your job is to see how he has chosen to develop it, in order to determine the sequence of his organization.

The author's *main point* is both the most important statement he makes about his subject, and the focus of his organization. It is the central idea of the article, around which everything else revolves. Try to phrase this idea as simply as possible, perhaps in a single sentence.

The main idea of the piece we've been discussing may be that students from schools with larger classes generally achieve higher (or lower) scores on national math tests. Or that students from rural schools typically do better (or worse) than those from urban schools. Or that none of these factors has any significant effect on test scores. The main point of his article may also be that such scores do (or do not) serve to predict future performance in math classes. Every well-written article normally has such a unifying central idea.

While making a preliminary survey you should *not* aim for full understanding. You're only seeking a general idea of the article as a whole. Much of the value of the initial survey lies in the questions it leaves *unanswered*, for these tell you what to look for in the readings that follow. The mere fact that you're able to ask intelligent questions indicates that the preliminary survey has done its job.

Techniques of the Preliminary Survey

The preliminary survey should be made as rapidly as possible by skimming through the material in search of key ideas. You should be able to do this at an average rate of at least 1000 WPM. A 5000-word magazine article should therefore take you no more than five minutes. Don't expect to *read* the entire piece in this time; simply scan it actively for general understanding. With a little practice most students readily learn to survey material at an average rate of well over 1000 WPM.

Don't worry about details or difficult passages. All you want is a clear idea of the author's subject, organization, and main point, and you should concentrate on these elements. Remember, though, that the preliminary survey shouldn't be aimless. You have to search alertly for the information you want.

To help you do this, you should pay particular attention to the parts of an article or chapter most likely to contain what you're looking for:

1. Title
2. Introduction
3. Paragraph topics
4. Transitions
5. Summary or conclusion
6. Mechanical devices of organization and emphasis.

Title. The title alone may tell you very little and even be misleading, but expository writers generally try to phrase a helpful title:

"What Makes Great Books Great?"
"What French Readers Find in William Faulkner's Fiction"
"College Athletics: Education or Show Business?"
"The Comedy of Charlie Chaplin"

Even a temporarily meaningless title can be of value in helping you frame some of the questions the article should answer.

Introduction. The introductory matter may be no more than a single sentence, or may run to several paragraphs. Don't look only for formal or stilted introductions:

In this article I am going to discuss . . . .

Professional writers usually prefer something less obvious, but in one way or another an introduction tells you just that—what the author is going to discuss.

Read, for instance, this title and opening paragraph from a magazine article:

BRANDEIS

On November 13, 1856, in Louisville, Kentucky, was born Louis Dembitz Brandeis, who can be fairly claimed to rank in influence upon American law second only to John Marshall. He was not the philosopher-poet that Holmes was; nor had he the range of scholarship or the purity of detachment which characterized Cardozo; and he was without the magisterial command that Hughes so magnificently embodied. Yet, even in company with those giants, Brandeis made the second long stride which gave American law a pace distinctive from, if responsive to, English jurisprudence.
Charles J. Wyzanski, Jr.

An alert reader can learn a great deal from this. Obviously, the subject of the article is Louis Brandeis or, more specifically, his legal career. The main point may deal with either his "influence upon American law" or his personal greatness. In the latter instance, his contributions to law may serve as illustration of his greatness. The author gives little indication of his intended organization but, even so, you should be able to make some informed guesses. He may, for instance, trace Brandeis' career, analyze his background and character, compare him with other great judges, or discuss his personal or legal philosophy.

A good reader will also note that this introduction has several obvious omissions. What was the "second long stride" in American legal history credited to Brandeis? What was the first, and who made it? What unique qualities of greatness did Brandeis possess? (The author mentions only those he did not possess.) These questions have been carefully urged upon you by the author. In finding their answers, you will probably also find the main point of the article.

Sometimes writers actually phrase the questions for you:

> Do our men like women as people? Are they really interested in the ideas, the points of view, the conversation of women? Are they responsive to women when the physical connotations inseparable from any relationship of the sexes are weak, as when one lunches with a woman beyond her physical prime but attractive because she is mellow, mature, stimulating? Do our men admit women to a rounded intimacy with them and treat them as equals, or do they keep them in a mink-lined purdah beyond which they are not permitted to go?
> David L. Cohn, "Do American Men Like Women?"

In his introduction an author usually provides clues to help you proceed intelligently. You should be ready to take advantage of whatever guidance he offers.

Paragraph Topics. Determine quickly the topic of each paragraph by skimming through it, looking for key words and phrases. Since the topic is often directly stated at the beginning or end, you can frequently survey by simply reading the first and last sentences of each paragraph.

(As a general rule, the most important parts of *all* units of writing—sentences, paragraphs, articles, chapters, and books—are the beginning and the end. You should always pay particular attention to these two places as the most likely sources of important material.)

Paragraphs of introduction, transition, and summary or conclusion should be given special emphasis. But even these can be largely skimmed, or perhaps read selectively, in your survey. In general, emphasize paragraphs that bring in new points, not paragraphs that explain or illustrate ideas that have already been stated. Don't worry if you miss the topics of some paragraphs. All you want is a sharp impression of the outlines of the work. You'll have time later for full understanding.

Transitions. A transition may be a word, a phrase, a sentence, a paragraph, or even several paragraphs. In each case it connects what has been said with what is going to be said.

Sometimes the transition is obvious:

> So much for the teaching of the understanding of international affairs. Now a word about the teaching of the practice of it.
> George F. Kennan, "Training for Statesmanship"

This is a full transition, clearly indicating what is finished and what is coming. But even a partial transition, in which the writer implies but does not state, can be useful:

> But there is also a deeper level to our uneasiness.
> Oscar Handlin, "Yearning for Security"

Obviously the author has just completed discussing *superficial* levels of uneasiness, even though he does not actually say so. An alert reading of one or two transitional sentences can thus give you the topics of several surrounding paragraphs. This kind of efficiency allows you to survey material quickly and skillfully.

Summary or Conclusion. A summary is a restatement of material already presented. A conclusion reflects the development of a new point that grows out of previous material. A summary points backward. A conclusion points forward. A writer may use one or the other, neither, or both in combination. They are usually found at or near the end of an article or chapter, most often in the last paragraph.

Sometimes an author clearly labels them:

> To summarize, in conclusion, thus we see, as a result, therefore, this leads us to believe that

Frequently he sets forth a precise condensation of the whole piece, to emphasize the points he considers most important:

> The novelists I have discussed in this Part see the issues of their day in terms of society's danger to life, that is, to the experience of the individual as something free, as something full of the possibilities of growth and choice and spontaneity. Whether it is the army organization, the business organization, or the middle-class social organization, the apparatus must be exposed as the danger it is. Their emphasis, therefore, is upon external conflict rather than psychological conflicts within the self....
> Jerry H. Bryant, *The Open Decision*

As with the introduction, you should also look for the reinforcement of major ideas through less direct methods of phrasing:

> The young, miserably educated as they are, bring with them almost nothing but healthy instincts. The project of building a sophisticated framework of thought atop those instincts is rather like trying to graft an oak tree upon a wildflower. How to sustain the oak tree? More important, how to avoid crushing the wildflower? And yet such is the project that confronts those of us who are concerned with radical social change....
> Theodore Roszak, *The Making of the Counter-Culture*

Instead of exposition or analysis, Roszak employs an *image* to illustrate his point.

In general, you should use the summary or conclusion to complete the overall understanding you have gained. By the time you reach this point in your survey, you should have a pretty good idea of the subject and organization of the article. But the main point, in many cases, is withheld until the end.

Mechanical Devices of Organization and Emphasis. Writers frequently divide their work into sections, and a glance at the section headings can give you an excellent preview of the subject and its organization. Even without headings, the sections are useful in that they reflect important divisions in the work.

Various mechanical devices are also used to emphasize important ideas within the organization. An author may, for instance, have key words or sentences printed in *italic* type, in **boldface** type, or in CAPITALS. He may present important points in a numbered list set apart from the normal paragraphing. Such enumerations serve to

1. Emphasize material
2. Simplify complicated material
3. Indicate organizational patterns

An author may also emphasize an idea with a short, one-sentence paragraph.

All such mechanical devices are consciously used by a writer to call attention to important material. Since your purpose in a preliminary survey is to discover as quickly as possible the most important elements within a mass of undifferentiated material, these devices are of great help.

Step 1b: Recapitulation

All three steps in the basic reading pattern are composed of two parts. In each case the second part is the *recapitulation*, in your mind, of everything you have learned. The time it takes can be measured in seconds, yet it's extremely important.

Immediately after your preliminary survey, mentally reconstruct all the material you remember. This reconstruction should be an active process, not merely a passive review of your impressions. Try to give material a unifying sense of order and emphasis. To recapitulate:

1. State the specific *subject* of the piece as fully and exactly as you can.
2. State the *main point* the author makes about the subject as fully and exactly as you can.
3. Reconstruct the *organization* of the piece, showing the step-by-step development of the subject and the main point and indicating clearly just what approach the author has taken to his material. Include everything of importance that you remember. Arrange the material as much as possible in proper sequence. Distinguish between major and minor points, or between potentially major and minor points.
4. Whenever you are unable to make statements, ask yourself questions. Note the gaps in your understanding and remind yourself to seek out the material you need to fill these gaps.

The recapitulation thus enables you to clarify and organize what you have learned and to determine what you still have to learn. It also prepares you to fit the detailed information you are about to receive into a coherent pattern.

EXERCISES

Recognizing Important Parts of an Article

1. Choose an article at random from a popular magazine. Working at your own speed, find and mark
   a. The introduction

    b. The summary or conclusion
    c. Mechanical devices of organization and emphasis.

   Select two consecutive pages from the article and mark
    a. All transitional material
    b. The topic sentence of each paragraph.

   If you cannot find a topic sentence, try to phrase one for yourself.

2. Choose another article and repeat the above exercise, working more rapidly. Do not read the article. Merely skim it rapidly, looking for the above material.

Making the Preliminary Survey

1. Choose *three* more articles. Make a preliminary survey and recapitulation of each. Even if you have difficulty at first, do not let your rate fall below an average of 1000 WPM. Approximate the number of words in each article and set a time limit for each survey. Try to improve your rate on each succeeding article by forcing yourself to survey it in less time. Concentrate on finding and phrasing the subject, organization, and main point.

2. Practice working with someone else to gain skill in phrasing ideas accurately. Choose an article and take turns surveying it rapidly. Phrase the results for each other to see how well you've done. If you disagree, evaluate each other's interpretation, referring back to the article if necessary. But don't feel obligated to agree precisely on everything. A variety of possible interpretations, if based on a perceptive survey, can be equally helpful.

3. Make a preliminary survey of the next chapter in this book. It's approximately 6000 words long and should be surveyed in about six minutes. Recapitulate and proceed to read it. Then decide whether the six minutes were worthwhile.

Chapter 5

A Basic Reading Pattern for Exposition: Details and Difficulties

You'll now be able to use the knowledge gained in your preliminary survey as a basis for the readings of the second and third steps.

Step 2a: Filling in Details

At this point you're ready to *expand, clarify,* and *correct* the information gathered in your survey. You'll do this by filling in details previously ignored and by trying to answer questions that arose during your recapitulation.

Techniques of Filling in Details

Read the article rapidly and alertly. Vary your speed according to the importance and complexity of different passages but always keep it at or above normal. Your *average* rate for the whole article should be 100 to 200 WPM faster than normal.

Skim rapidly over, or skip, material you understand adequately from your survey. Always be alert, though, to correct misconceptions and to improve your understanding of important points.

Skim rapidly over, or skip, unimportant passages. You may consider something unimportant if it has no interest or value for you, or if, on the basis of your survey, you decide it bears an insignificant relation to the author's subject.

Search out key passages. Give particular emphasis once more to the title, the introduction, paragraph topics, transitions, the summary or conclusion, and mechanical devices of organization and emphasis.

Fit details into broad patterns. Keep the writer's main point and organization in mind and fit all new material into this pattern. Distinguish between important and unimportant details. Try to determine the interrelationship of everything you learn.

Do not go back to reread difficult passages if you cannot grasp their meaning in a single rapid reading. You may want to mark these passages for later attention.

Do not look up unfamiliar words. If you cannot figure out their meaning from the context, mark them for future attention.

To achieve detailed knowledge while reading faster than normal, you should recognize and respond to the techniques commonly used by expository writers to present their material:

1. Direct statement
2. Definition
3. Question
4. Comparison and contrast
5. Example and illustration

Direct Statement. A writer of exposition often directly states important ideas:

> The three main causes of labor disputes are....
> The basic problem of U.S. foreign policy is....

Surprisingly, many readers overlook such obvious presentations of key points.

Definition. A careful writer generally defines important or unusual terms, or terms that he is using in a precise, scientific sense:

> Protozoa, as we all know, are one-celled creatures, and their history must date from the first billion years of emergent life. One kind of protozoa are known as slime molds. They are of the size and general appearance of a white blood cell, and they feed on bacteria such as one finds in moist soil. They divide every three or four hours, and so a population multiplies rapidly. Just about the time, however, when growing numbers have exhausted the food supply in a given area, the single-cell creatures enter the second phase of their life cycle. They begin to form societies. Around a founder cell others will bunch in a growing aggregate, clinging together until they have formed a sausage-shaped slug visible to the naked eye. Now this social slug of individual beings begins to behave as a single organism, and will even move toward warmth or toward light with precision of direction. At last a portion of the community will differentiate themselves and form a stalk which they stiffen with a secretion. Then others will crawl on top of the stalk and form a sphere of cells each containing a spore, the seed of a new generation.
> Robert Ardrey, *The Territorial Imperative*

Ardrey defines the term "slime mold" with a rather extensive life history of the organism. He could have simply said, "The slime mold is a form of protozoa." A skillful writer defines terms to the extent that the reader needs such a definition. You can thus often tell how important a concept is by the care with which the author defines it.

Many writers also define vague or abstract words —love, morality, success—to indicate the particular meaning they intend.

> Were they pressed hard enough, most men would probably confess that political freedom—that is to say, the right to speak freely and to act in opposition—is a noble idea rather than a practical necessity.
> Walter Lippman, "The Indispensable Opposition"

Question. As noted earlier, a writer frequently poses a question and then proceeds to answer it. Such questions almost always signal the introduction of major ideas and set forth the topic of subsequent passages:

> Who were the pioneers? Who were the men who left their homes and went into the wilderness? A man rarely leaves a soft spot and goes deliberately in search of hardship and privation. People become attached to the places they live in; they drive roots. A change of habitat is a painful act of uprooting. A man who has made good and has a standing in his community stays put. The successful businessmen, farmers and workers usually stayed where they were. Who then left for the wilderness and the unknown? Obviously those who had not made good: men who went broke or never amounted to much; men who though possessed of abilities were too impulsive to stand the daily grind; men who were slaves of their appetites—drunkards, gamblers, and woman-chasers; outcasts—fugitives from justice and ex-jailbirds. There were no doubt some who went in search of health—men suffering with TB, asthma, heart trouble. Finally there was a sprinkling of young and middle-aged in search of adventure.
> Eric Hoffer, "The Role of the Undesirables"

Comparison and Contrast. When dealing with material that may be unfamiliar to his readers, a writer may try to clarify it by comparing or contrasting it to something they already know:

> Light, in the latest theory, is not waves in a sea of ether, or a jet from a nozzle; it could be compared rather to machine gun fire, every photoelectric bullet of energy travelling in a regular rhythm....
> Donald Culross Peattie, "The Flowering Earth"

A writer may also use a comparison or contrast to show differences between familiar concepts:

> ... The pattern of man's existence is fairly simple. He is born; he is educated partly to be a person and partly to earn a living; he earns a living, gets a wife, begets children, and works until he dies. The pattern of a woman's life today is essentially different. After she graduates from college she is faced with her first major choice: family or career (although "career" is a glamour word for the kind of jobs most women can get!). If a man marries he must work harder than ever at his career; there is no conflict. Yet, despite all the brave phrases which are currently fashionable, a married woman who tries to combine the two usually has either a token career or a token family, at least so long as her children are young.
> Lynn White, Jr., "Educating Women in a Man's World"

Example and Illustration. In the following passage, the first sentence makes a general comment relating to the "decay of services in general." The rest of the paragraph contains supporting examples:

But if the car owner can ignore the lack of public transport, he can hardly ignore the decay of services in general. His car needs mechanics, and mechanics grow more expensive and less efficient. The gadgets in the home are cheaper to replace than repair. The more efficiently self-contained the home, primary fortress of independence, seems to be, the more dependent it is on the great impersonal corporations, as well as a diminishing army of servitors. Skills at the lowest level have to be wooed slavishly and exorbitantly rewarded. Plumbers will not come. Nor, at the higher level, will doctors. And doctors and dentists, in a nation committed to maiming itself with sugar and cholesterol, know their scarcity value and behave accordingly.

Anthony Burgess, "Is America Falling Apart?"

The *direct statement* and the *definition* are the basic methods of exposition. The most significant points are generally stated or defined directly. The *question* is usually important insofar as it leads you to an answer, probably presented as a direct statement or definition. The *comparison and contrast* and the *example and illustration* are generally used not to make a point, but to support or explain it.

Naturally the list given above is not complete, for an expository writer may also develop his ideas through a story, a joke, or a veiled implication. He may also employ metaphors, similes, images, or symbols, as in Roszak's reference to an oak tree and a wildflower. Some of these additional techniques are discussed in later chapters, as they are more common in persuasive and imaginative writing.

Step 2b: Recapitulation

Immediately after your reading to fill in details, mentally reconstruct everything you remember:

1. State as fully as you can your expanded and perhaps revised version of the author's *subject* and *main point*.
2. Reconstruct the *organization* of the article, showing the step-by-step development of the subject and main point. Include everything of importance that you remember. Try to arrange material in the proper sequence and to indicate relative degrees of importance. Look for interrelationships.
3. Whenever you are uncertain about an important point, *ask yourself questions*.

After a little practice, most students can understand articles of moderate difficulty as fully as they wish at this point. We assume, though, that there remain unanswered questions and elements of uncertainty. In this case, the recapitulation again serves, as it did in step 1, to indicate the emphasis and objectives of your subsequent reading.

Step 3a: Clearing Up Difficulties

Up to now your readings have been performed under pressure. You surveyed at over 1000 WPM and filled in details at 100 to 200 WPM above normal. These rates should always remain at least that high, regardless of the difficulty of the material.

Step 3 lets you adjust your reading time to the demands of the material. It can be as brief or as lengthy as you wish. Often this reading can be eliminated or take only a minute or two. For extremely difficult or complex works, it may take hours.

But the absence of a time limit shouldn't encourage you to become passive or aimless. Clear up difficulties as quickly as possible by means of alert reading. Your objective now is to understand the article as fully as you desire by concentrating on the obscure or difficult passages you have not yet mastered.

Techniques of Clearing Up Difficulties

Do not reread passages you already understand. You should have a relatively thorough knowledge of the article at this point and should be able to skip most of it.

Reread at a normal or faster-than-normal rate passages that have given you trouble. Remember that even at this stage several fast readings are usually more effective than a single slow one.

Study intensively anything of importance that you still do not fully understand. Try to relate the troublesome passages to the overall pattern of the article. All important material should bear a meaningful relationship to the author's organization and main point.

Make another attempt to determine from their context the meanings of unfamiliar words that you marked earlier. Your more complete knowledge of the whole article should help you. If your efforts are unsuccessful, look up in a dictionary words that are (1) necessary for the understanding of important passages or (2) partially familiar to you, indicating that you have met them before.

Step 3b: Recapitulation

After you have satisfactorily understood everything of importance, make a final recapitulation of what you have learned. This recapitulation is not, like the other, designed to prepare you for a subsequent reading, but to help you better understand *and remember* what you have read.

1. State your final version of the author's *subject* and *main point*.
2. Reconstruct your final version of the *organization*, showing the step-by-step development of

the subject and main point. Include everything of significance, indicating relative degrees of importance.
3. Make sure you've answered all the questions from your previous recapitulation. If you discover flaws in your understanding, return once more to the appropriate passages.

At this stage, you should have achieved a full understanding of the writer's exposition, reflected in a thorough and organized recapitulation.

READING BOOK-LENGTH EXPOSITION

The basic reading pattern needs only minor variations in the preliminary survey for use on book-length exposition.

Surveying a Book

You can survey a 300-page book of exposition in ten or fifteen minutes. Try to discover the author's subject, organization, and main point through an alert analysis of the

1. Title
2. Table of contents
3. Dust jacket information (if available)

and through a rapid skimming of the

4. Preface, foreword, or introduction
5. First chapter
6. Transitional passages at the beginning and end of chapters or sections
7. Last chapter

A book naturally has a broader subject and main point than an article, and a more complex organization. In many cases, there may be several subjects and main points of equal importance. But you should learn enough from a quick survey and recapitulation to begin reading with intelligence and foresight. Once again you do not need, and should not expect, fullness or certainty from the preliminary survey.

Two Basic Approaches

After your survey, decide which of two basic approaches you wish to use in subsequent readings. The first treats the book as a collection of short articles. The second treats it as a single article of great length.

With the first approach, you'll work for a full understanding of each chapter before going to the next. You'll do this by using *all three steps* of the basic reading pattern on each chapter in turn, as you would on a series of articles. This approach is probably better for the reading of textbooks, or of any book that is demanding or that is of real interest or importance to you. You will normally cover only a short section of such books at each sitting, yet will want excellent comprehension of the material.

With the second approach, you'll only survey and fill in details for a chapter before going to the next one. The intensive work of the third unit—clearing up difficulties—will be withheld until you have finished reading the whole book in this manner, at which time it can be applied to the whole book or to selected portions. This approach is better suited to lighter or less important books which probably will not have many difficulties to clear up.

Reading Chapters

Since chapters, unlike articles, are interrelated parts of a larger work, you should give special emphasis in surveys and readings to transitional material at the beginning and end of each chapter. These transitions will help you to discover the essential unity among the different parts of the book.

Recapitulations

You should pause after every chapter to recapitulate its contents. If you read a book in several sittings, as you normally will, develop the habit of rapidly recapitulating important previous material each time you resume reading. Your final recapitulation, naturally, will take place after you have finished the book.

Resurveying a Book

The best way to understand and remember the contents of a book is to begin and end with a survey. The final resurvey is performed in the same manner as the preliminary survey and should take only ten or fifteen minutes. You can resurvey a book as soon as you finish it, or a few days, a week, or even a month later. In general, a resurvey is most effective when performed at least several days after you finish reading, although of course it is better to do it right away than not at all. The few minutes spent on a resurvey will greatly improve your understanding and retention of material.

VALUE OF THE BASIC READING PATTERN

Despite its apparent length when explained in detail, the basic reading pattern is actually quite streamlined and efficient, requiring no additional time for the reading of a given work. For example, assume your normal reading rate is 300 WPM. A single ordinary reading of a 6000-word article would take twenty minutes. Using the basic reading pattern, you would spend:

1. Making a preliminary survey,
   6000 words at 1000 WPM   6 minutes
2. Filling in details,
   6000 words at 500 WPM
   (200 WPM above normal)   12 minutes
                          Total   18 minutes

This leaves you two minutes for the recapitulations, which should be sufficient for an article of this length.

In the time you would have spent on a single ordinary reading, you are instead able to survey the material, recapitulate, read to fill in details, and again recapitulate. (And with practice, you will be able to work even faster, especially as both your base rate and your surveying speed increase. A rate of 1000 WPM, for instance, should be considered only a minimum for surveying.)

Although most material can be satisfactorily read with just these first two units, more difficult pieces naturally require the intensive work of the third unit. Yet the same material would also require additional time under an ordinary system of reading. And because the amount of time needed for a given piece of reading depends on your efficiency as a reader, the basic reading pattern actually saves time by teaching you to be more efficient.

USE OF THE BASIC READING PATTERN

The reading pattern we have set up requires the habitual use of good techniques. But it is *not* designed to make your habits inflexible. A good reader is versatile. He knows that different types of material must be read in different ways, and that as his purpose in reading changes so must his techniques.

We have assumed that your purpose in reading exposition is simply to achieve good comprehension. But the concept of comprehension (from the Latin *comprehendere*, meaning "to seize, to grasp, to capture"—reemphasizing the aggressiveness that characterizes good reading) can bear examination. What, specifically, makes for good comprehension?

How much does it depend on an understanding of the writer's main point? His organization? His techniques? His vocabulary? His minor points? His examples and illustrations? And what about some of the elements we have left for future discussion: What about the writer's purpose? His tone and mood? His attitudes?

Naturally, some understanding of all of these is needed, but in what proportion? Who has the superior comprehension, a reader who understands the main point but is hazy about details, or one who grasps numerous details but is uncertain of the basic idea? And how good is a reader who understands both main points and details but seriously misinterprets the writer's purpose or attitude? Or one who understands well while reading but quickly forgets everything? Or one who remembers well but without any sense of relative importance?

Almost all students have gone into an examination confident of their mastery of the material, only to discover that they studied the wrong things. In one sense, their comprehension of the material was excellent. In another sense, it was demonstrably inadequate.

In reading, as in studying, "good comprehension" can be defined as *the kind of comprehension you desire*. As a skilled reader you should always be able to obtain what you want.

The basic reading pattern enables you to do this. The separate units can be used with whatever emphasis and in whatever combination you desire. You should freely extract from this system the techniques you need for each reading occasion, without regard to their position in the various units.

You may, for instance, feel that certain material does not need a preliminary survey. In that case, you can begin with the second unit. If the material is easy to understand, you may also decide to eliminate the third unit. But in your single reading you should not hesitate to use whatever appropriate techniques of the other units you need.

After a while, you should find yourself improvising easily and automatically, for you will have freed yourself from the life-long habit of reading everything—from casual articles of remote interest to works of great importance and value—in the same slow, inefficient, and unvarying manner.

EXERCISES

The following exercises will give you the immediate practice you need. The best way, however, to become expert in using this system is simply to begin using it, with appropriate variations, for *all your reading*.

Reading Articles

Read three articles from a magazine or college reader, using on each in turn all three units of the basic reading pattern, including the recapitulations. Time yourself for the first two units to make certain you survey at over 1000 WPM and read to fill in details at 100 to 200 WPM faster than normal. On the basis of your final recapitulations, judge whether you have done a better job on the third article than on the first.

Reading a Magazine

Choose an issue of a magazine that you think you will enjoy. Read the issue from cover to cover in one sitting, using the techniques of the basic reading pattern on a selective basis. Make a preliminary survey of each article, but proceed to subsequent readings only when the article merits them on the basis of interest or difficulty. In other words, use only the units you need for each piece. When you finish, you should have a general impression of all the articles (from your surveys), a relatively full comprehension of some articles (from filling in details), and an exhaustive comprehension of at least a few articles (from clearing up difficulties).

This gives you valuable practice in flexible use of the basic reading pattern. It also shows you how you can read a great deal more than you now do, with *as much comprehension as you desire.*

Reading a Book

Select a short (200 to 300 pages) expository book that you think will be interesting. Read the entire book in one sitting, using the techniques of the basic reading pattern. Make a preliminary survey of the whole work. Then use the second and third steps on individual chapters as needed or desired. In this manner, you should gain a good understanding of the book as a whole and an excellent understanding of selected portions. Equally important, you will prove to yourself that you can often read a book in one sitting with as much comprehension as you wish, and probably more than you used to achieve.

Note: A great value of this system is that it encourages you to *read more.* Using it, you know that you must spend on your reading only as much time as the material deserves. Thus reading is never drudgery and never unrewarding.

Reading the Rest of This Book

Follow the basic reading pattern in reading the remainder of this book:

1. Make a preliminary survey of the portion that remains, as you would survey a whole book.
2. Make a preliminary survey of the next chapter. It is about 9000 words long and should be surveyed in about nine minutes. Recapitulate and then read to fill in details at 100 to 200 WPM above your normal rate. Again recapitulate and return to clear up difficulties. Then make a final recapitulation. Judge for yourself whether you have a better understanding of that chapter than of previous ones.
3. Follow the same approach for each of the succeeding chapters in turn. When you finish the book, make a final recapitulation of the entire work.

Chapter 6
Writing Exposition

The preceding chapters treated the structure and content that a good reader looks for in exposition. Your task, as a writer of exposition, is to provide the qualities you would look for as a reader. Writing is the other side of the coin, and a person who knows how to read effectively has already taken a big step toward becoming a better writer.

In this chapter we'll set forth a basic writing pattern for exposition, using the same principles as the reading pattern. It will encourage you to work from the general to the particular, to separate the writing process into distinct steps, and to work actively toward well-defined goals. It is also designed, like the reading pattern, to be adapted freely to your individual needs.

The writing you do of course varies a great deal. You may be given a specific assignment or left to choose your own. Sometimes you're expected to write under the pressure of class or test conditions, while other times you may have several weeks for an assignment. Your paper may be technical or scholarly, and thus based on extensive research, or may derive solely from your personal experiences and observations. Rather than attempting to cover all these possible variations, or such technical matters as library research, we'll concentrate on the writing process itself. We'll assume therefore that you possess the information needed for your paper, having gained it through either research or personal experience.

This chapter deals only with expository writing, to take advantage of what you've learned in the preceding chapter about reading exposition. Again we assume that you are writing *pure* exposition even though, as we've noted, writers usually have mixed purposes.

(In Chapter 8, following the section on reading persuasion, we'll treat persuasive writing. In Chapter 10, after our discussion of the reading of fiction, poetry, and drama, we'll set forth some guidelines to help you in writing about these literary works.)

To write good exposition, you must have something to say, must put the words down on paper, and must be able to make your presentation effective. The process can thus be broken down into three stages:

1. Formulating your ideas
2. Producing a first draft
3. Producing a final draft

FORMULATING YOUR IDEAS

Once you possess the information you need, you can begin by formulating as clearly and fully as possible the same three elements you would look for, as a reader, in a preliminary survey of a piece of exposition: the subject, the main point, and the organization.

Although some people can "work in their heads," it's generally preferable to write brief notes as part of your preparation. These help clarify your ideas and can later serve as a tentative outline for the first draft.

Start by phrasing as precisely as possible the *subject* of your intended paper. As in your reading, try to make this specific. "The United Nations" is obviously too broad. "The administrative structure of the United Nations" is better. "The powers of the secretary-general of the United Nations" is better still: more exact, more limited, and more fully stated. Of all the possible papers on a given subject, you want to indicate as precisely as possible the paper *you* intend to write.

The same is true of a more personal paper. Try to avoid such catch-all statements of your subject as "My childhood" or "Outdoor sports." Work toward a specific and concrete statement—"the challenge of white-water canoeing," for instance, rather than "outdoor sports." A long paper may require a broader subject than a short one. But don't choose a vague subject; try to keep it narrowly defined.

You can then try to write down a clear statement of the *main point* of the paper, which should be the most important thing you have to say about your subject. Since we're assuming that the paper is purely expository, your main point will most likely be informative, an outgrowth of the factual material and not simply an expression of your personal views.

Based on your reading and research, for instance, your main point may be that the powers of the secretary-general are broad and expansive, that they're rigidly limited, or that they depend largely on the personal and political qualities of the officeholder.

Based on your subject and main point, you can then list briefly the secondary ideas you intend to include, their number and complexity depending on the length of the paper. You can list them as they occur to you, without worrying about their order or relative importance. This allows for freer exploration of the subject and often produces valuable ideas which a more careful ordering might cause you to overlook.

You can then reconsider the list, adding whatever is needed and weeding out anything that seems irrelevant or unnecessary. Next, you can arrange the items in a tentative order which can serve as a rough outline of your *organization*. These points of course should support your main idea and should be closely related to it. Ideally, the sum of all your secondary points should add up to the full statement of your main point.

Your planning will not always proceed this smoothly or in this order. Sometimes you'll find it more natural to begin by listing secondary ideas, working from them to a determination of your main point or to a more precise statement of your subject. You should use whatever method seems to work best, as long as you spend a reasonable amount of time and thought *preparing* to write.

This holds true even when time is very short. When assigned an in-class paper, many students plunge immediately into the writing so as not to waste any time. This is usually a mistake. Even two or three minutes spent organizing your thoughts and jotting down key points can be a great help.

When you have several days or a week for a paper, it's good to do some preliminary work as soon as possible. On the day you receive the assignment, for instance, write out some rough notes about your subject, main point, and organization. Even if you don't look at them for a few days, they'll start you thinking about the paper and give you a better idea of what has to be done.

PRODUCING THE FIRST DRAFT

Work from your notes without being restricted by them. Your preliminary notes should aid you in getting started, but your best ideas will sometimes come as you write. Always feel free to depart from your plans, adding or deleting as the situation warrants.

Work in short, concentrated stretches. Many people work best when they set aside a specific period of time for their first draft. Instead of vaguely planning to do the work "tonight," give yourself an hour, set a realistic goal, and try to work without interruption. Working under a bit of pressure encourages you to stick to the job because you have no time to waste.

For a short paper you may want to complete the first draft in a single sitting. Long papers should probably be divided into smaller units. If you think a rough draft of a lengthy paper will take four hours, you may find it most efficient to work in four separate segments of one hour each.

(In general, you'll probably do best by devoting several short work sessions to a paper rather than trying to do everything, from first notes to final draft, in one long sitting. This will let you resume each time with a more objective view of what you've accomplished so far and a better idea of how to proceed.)

Suspend, for the moment, your critical instincts. Students frequently have trouble putting words down because they're too fussy at the wrong time. Remind yourself that the first draft is for you alone and that no one else need ever see it. It is not a permanent commitment but merely a trial run, and will obviously have things wrong with it.

The rough draft should allow you to write with as much natural flow as possible. You can accomplish this by concentrating on ideas and not worrying too much about the correctness or effectiveness of your phrasing. These matters are important, but there'll be time for them later. An overly critical attitude at this point may only inhibit the development of your ideas.

Phrase your thoughts simply and directly. Try to state your ideas in a simple and straightforward manner without attempting to "dress them up" in fine language. If you ideas are clearly formed, you should have little trouble phrasing them.

If you do have trouble, it may result from the fuzziness of the thought rather than from a lack of ability in phrasing. It's almost impossible to state clearly an idea that is not in itself clear. When you can't seem to put an idea down, try to phrase it as simply as possible, as if explaining it to someone in conversation. Once you can formulate it in your mind, you should be able to incorporate it in the first draft. The phrasing can always be polished later.

As a general rule, the simpler you keep the first draft, the fewer mistakes you'll have to correct afterward.

Make your rough draft slightly longer than needed. If the assignment calls for 500 words, aim for 600. This will let you approach the final draft without feeling compelled to keep every word. Then it will be a lot easier to eliminate weak or irrelevant sections and to compress your writing as needed.

PRODUCING A FINAL DRAFT

Ideally, a final draft should receive at least as much time as a rough draft. Professional writers generally give it a great deal more, often producing five or ten intermediate drafts before the final one. Students rarely need to devote that much effort to a piece of writing. But it's important to recognize the value of revision, and to give it the attention it deserves.

Your job at this stage is first to evaluate and then to improve your rough draft in order to produce a satisfactory final draft. Again, your best guide as a writer of exposition can be found in the qualities you most appreciate as a reader:

1. Intelligent and well-organized *content*
2. Clear and compressed *style*
3. Correct *mechanics*

You'll probably find it most effective to concentrate on each of these areas in turn, and in the order listed. This will let you work from the broad questions of content down to the specific details of mechanics. The basic decisions—what to include, and where, and in what proportion—are thus made before you spend time polishing and correcting individual passages. It's hardly worthwhile, after all, to perfect your first paragraph before you've decided whether you even want to keep it in the paper.

Content

The ideas expressed in your rough draft can be evaluated by referring once more to the most important structural elements: the subject, the main point, and the organization.

Does a reading of the paper, for instance, allow you clearly to define its *subject*? Do all your points relate to this subject or have you occasionally wandered from it? If you have, you should now decide whether these digressions should be more clearly related to the subject or simply eliminated.

You'll also want to see whether—given the length of the paper—you've treated the subject fully. If you've left out anything of importance, you can add it at this time.

Having cut and added as you've seen fit, you should then determine whether the *main point* of the paper is clear. Is it directly stated anywhere? If not, is it sufficiently implied? Has it been presented, either directly or by implication, with enough emphasis to distinguish it from less important points?

Remember that the main point—like everything else in your paper—should be clear not only to you but also to your readers. Try to evaluate what you've actually said, not merely what you intended to say.

With respect to *organization*, it's often helpful to write down briefly the topic of each paragraph. This gives you a skeletal outline which can reveal a good deal about the effectiveness of the organization. It also indicates something about the paragraphs themselves. If you have trouble finding the central idea of certain paragraphs, or discover that some seem overcrowded, disorganized, or underdeveloped, you will probably want to revise them.

Another way to test your organization is to rearrange, in your mind, the order of the paragraphs.

Would the paper suffer if the second and fifth paragraphs were interchanged? In a well-structured essay, any such change would normally destroy the logical sequence. If, however, certain paragraphs can be moved about without causing problems, it's a good sign that something may be wrong with your logical sequence.

Again, the key parts of an article that you sought as a reader should receive special attention from you as a writer:

1. Title
2. Introduction
3. Beginnings and ends of paragraphs
4. Transitions
5. Summary or conclusion
6. Mechanical devices of organization and emphasis

Does your title, for instance, help the reader understand your paper? Does it engage his interest and encourage him to read on? Does your introduction indicate the scope and purpose of the paper? Do your paragraphs tend to begin and end with important ideas?

Go through the rough draft specifically to check the transitions. In general, the bigger the "jump" between one point and the next, the more you'll need some sort of transition. If the ideas follow each other closely and logically, a transition is often unnecessary.

If your paper has a *summary* or a *conclusion*, ask yourself whether it's clear, whether it accurately reflects the material preceding it, and whether it's useful to the reader. You don't always need a summary or conclusion. Often the best way to end a short, straightforward paper is simply to stop after you've made your final point. Even when a closing statement seems called for, it can frequently be quite brief.

Enumeration, indented lists, underlining, section headings, and other *mechanical devices of emphasis and organization* are aids for the reader and generally ought to be employed only when clearly needed. A long paper divided into several parts may well benefit from the use of section headings. A short treatment of a single idea hardly seems to require them.

Before moving on to other considerations, you should evaluate one more aspect of your organization: the proportions of your paper. It's easy to get carried away in a rough draft, and you may have gone on excessively about a relatively minor point. At the same time you may have treated an important idea too skimpily. Your informal list of paragraph topics can guide you in judging the proportions of your paper. How much space, for instance, have you spent on introductory and concluding material, as opposed to the main idea and its supporting points?

During this revision of the paper's content, you should do whatever is necessary in the way of adding, eliminating, and rearranging material. You should make sure that your subject is unified, your main point clearly presented, and your organization logical. Having thus satisfied yourself with the paper's content, you can turn your attention to the effectiveness of its style and finally to the correctness of its mechanics.

Style

Your style is a constantly developing reflection of your intelligence, perceptions, command of the language, sensitivity, interests, attitudes, experiences, and probably a great deal more. It's as unique as you are, as individual as your mind, your voice, your appearance, your posture, or your gestures. As such, its characteristics are to some extent beyond your control but, like other attributes you possess, they can be significantly modified through learning. Although the *quality* of your voice is probably inherited, for instance, you can nonetheless learn to speak more clearly.

You can improve your writing style most significantly by aiming for two things: *clarity* and *compression*. There are of course other virtues—gracefulness, subtlety, variety, forcefulness, originality, intensity, etc. But these cannot realistically be achieved until you have first mastered the two basic attributes of a good expository style. If you can write clearly and concisely, you have eliminated most of the problems that plague students and have gone a long way toward developing an effective style.

Clarity

In discussing the rough draft, we suggested that you strive for simplicity and directness. The same holds true for the final draft. This is not to suggest that you reduce everything to a kind of simple-minded diagram or that you avoid complex subjects. But your writing is likely to suffer far more from needless clutter than from excessive simplicity. You can try too hard to impress the reader—and the instructor—by "dressing up" your writing in the hope it will seem somehow better than it actually is.

There's a pretension involved in this which robs the writing of honesty. The harder you try to impress others, the less impressive your writing becomes. Your goal as a writer should be to state essential matters clearly and honestly—without decoration, pretense, or needless complication. Most ideas can, and should, be stated simply.

Let's begin by taking a look at a few examples of good professional exposition:

> I do not enjoy unanimity. I suffer from crowd emotion, and resent it. So I had not been too happy under the impact of communal enthusiasm. Besides, I dislike pageants. They are as much a fake as forged pictures, and the descendants of ancient houses who dress up as their forbears have little in common with them except clothes.
>
> Bernard Berenson, *Seeing and Knowing*

> The number of books of poetry that are published each quarter on both sides of the Atlantic is now so great that only a small quantity of them ever receive adequate attention from reviewers. Moreover, as some of these volumes are by authors whose names command instantaneous public attention, the work of younger poets is often ignored in all save a few periodicals.
>
> Robin Skelton, "Comment," in *The Malahat Review*

> A nation cannot exchange its national idea for a newer model any more than it can exchange its territories or population. The idea is the nation. It came on the *Mayflower*. It was alive before the first settlers crossed the Alleghenies. It has been bred into every generation. To change it, however compelling the reasons may seem, is to lose it; and to lose it is to lose the nation. If the American idea dissolves altogether there may still be an organized society occupying the North American continent, but it will not be America, whatever it is called. Since the American idea is of continual movement toward a significant and worthy future purpose, it cannot be contained in policies of defense and self-protection any more than in the denial of justice and narrowing of opportunity.
>
> Richard N. Goodwin, *The American Condition*

> Traveling the Great Lakes by birch-bark canoe was risky business. The canoes that carried men and supplies were exceedingly frail and would inevitably be twisted into fragments if they were caught in rough water. Inasmuch as the lakes can be as vicious as the North Atlantic when the winds come up, this meant that the expedition had to stay close to the shore all the way, running into the beach and hauling the canoes up beyond the reach of the surf whenever the breezes stiffened.
>
> Bruce Catton, *Waiting for the Morning Train*

These passages are direct and unpretentious, and they are clear. Nothing is faked, and nothing is dressed up. Good expository writing conveys information clearly and accurately and is successful—and impressive—only insofar as it does this.

The most common enemies of clarity are *pomposity, vagueness,* and *inaccuracy,* and these are faults you should avoid in your final draft.

Pomposity. A pompous person has an exaggerated sense of his own importance, which he often tries to support by showy pretenses in dress, speech, or manner. Pompous writing is likewise an attempt to make simple ideas seem profound or elegant through overblown phrasing.

Inflated writing thrives in business, in government, in the military, and at all levels of education and scholarship. President Franklin Roosevelt once advised a bureaucrat to tell his staff to "put out the lights" rather than "exterminate the illumination." The fact that so much pompous writing comes from organizations and "offices" rather than persons suggests one of its major faults: it lacks individuality. It's as lively and personal as a love letter written by a committee. Thus businessmen may speak of a "maximized degree of marketability potential," and scholars write sentences like:

> Singer . . . has proposed that capability and intentions are multiplicatively related and, like utility, refer to the probability of the source's intentions and the amount of cost or gains involved, based on the perceived capability of the source.

Student examples are just as easy to come by:

> The people who compose the immediate environment of my home town have continually on exhibition a premium display of various characteristics and traits.

> Some people are born content with their basic socioeconomic conditions as the prime factors contributing to their goals, and therefore never make a sufficient exertion to undertake more complex forms of existence.

Beneath the puffed-up language—and the confusion and grammatical dislocations that so often accompany it—there exists in each case a relatively straightforward idea:

> The people in my town display various traits.

> Some people are satisfied with what they have.

Neither of these briefer versions is very good. They're still too vague to communicate much, which illustrates the ultimate emptiness of most pompous writing. If you find sentences like this in your writing, first try to reduce them to as few words as possible. Then ask yourself whether or not they really say anything. If, as in these cases, the content is so vague as to be meaningless, you should either eliminate the sentences or make them concrete enough to convey some meaning. The real failing of pompous writing is that it serves only to camouflage a lack of thought.

Vagueness. Vague writing, like pompous writing, usually results from a lack of precision in the writer's thinking, or phrasing, or both:

> His room is not unusual, or unlike other rooms. But the furniture is a mixture of old and new and gives the room some unknown or perhaps undefined quality.
>
> Back in early times, the need for censorship was just as great as it is today. However, due to the mores of the people and the influence of the society on each individual, means of entertainment were more or less censored on their own.

If you find passages like this in your own work, try to phrase the idea clearly and precisely in your mind. If you have trouble doing so, perhaps you haven't yet thought it through. The idea itself has to be clear before you can state it with any precision.

If the problem lies in the phrasing, try to remove words that are themselves so vague as to be incapable of precise communication:

> Not unusual, or unlike other rooms . . . some unknown or perhaps undefined quality . . . the mores of the people . . . back in early times . . .

What period, for instance, does "back in early times" refer to—the 1920s, the eighteenth century, the Middle Ages, the age of Greece? Surely the passage would have been clearer if the student had written:

> Back in the 1920s, the need for some form of censorship was just as great as it is today. However, due to the strong family ties of the day, the great influence of the church in defining acceptable patterns of behavior, and the conventional moral attitudes of small town life, there was less need for formal government censorship of books and movies.

In an effective essay, these ideas would still need to be developed further through specific details and illustrations, since they are only general assertions which have not been adequately supported. But the passage now gives the reader a much more accurate idea of the writer's subject and of his attitude toward it.

The tendency to rely on *abstract*, rather than *concrete*, expressions is perhaps the main cause of vague writing. Abstract terms generally refer to broad, fuzzy concepts that prompt highly individual reactions: "love," "honor," "duty," "freedom." We feel we know what the words mean, but these meanings are difficult to make clear to others. The same holds true for abstract words that allow us to make value judgments: "good," "bad," "decent," "fair," "unfair." These summarizing words express attitudes and state conclusions but are of little value in dealing with the reasoning behind them.

To write:

> I believe that the laws relating to welfare benefits are unfair

may allow you to express your feelings about the subject, but doesn't by itself communicate much to the reader. In what ways are the laws unfair? Do they allow too many or too few people to receive benefits? Do they provide too much or too little support? Are they unfair to the recipients or to someone else?

Concrete terms, on the other hand, convey meaning accurately because people can agree on their meaning. Something is concrete when we can respond to it with one of our five senses. It is something we can see, hear, touch, smell, or taste. "A house," "an automobile," "$20,000," and "one year," are concrete terms. "I would like to own a house and an automobile and make $20,000 a year," communicates much more than "I would like to live a comfortable life."

There are of course levels of abstraction and concreteness. "A house" and "an automobile" are certainly concrete, but "a two-story colonial" and "a Rolls-Royce" are even more so. How much concrete detail you should use is a matter of judgment on your part. It is hardly necessary to give the dimensions of every room in the house or to list all the options on the car. Common sense indicates that neither too little nor too much detail is desirable. You need enough to be clear, but not so much that it becomes burdensome.

Inaccuracy. It's not always easy to find the precise word you need. Language lacks scientific exactitude. As a writer, though, it's your responsibility to choose words that convey your meaning as accurately as possible. Consider the following excerpt from a student paper:

> Most people fail to recognize the importance of ambition. It is, after all, a prerequisite for existence.

Both "prerequisite" and "existence" are poorly chosen. A prerequisite is something that is required, a necessary preliminary for something else. It's unlikely that the writer believes that ambition is a requirement for existence. Whatever he meant to say, his careless choice of words has prevented him from making it clear. You should be on the lookout for words whose meaning you are not sure of and that you may have used inappropriately.

You won't usually be able to improve your phrasing by resorting to unfamiliar or exotic words. Nor does it help to load down your writing with additional qualifiers and involved explanations. You can best develop an accurate style by using words that are natural to you, by simplifying your sentence structure, and by using concrete terms whenever possible.

Compression

After you've done what you can to make your writing clear, you should work toward the second characteristic of good style: compression. You should be both as clear and as brief as you can.

You must especially guard against a continuing pattern of wordiness. In exposition, words serve as a means of transmitting ideas. The *pace* of your writing is thus determined by the *proportion of words to ideas*. A paper is not wordy simply because it is long. A paper becomes wordy when the length is not justified by the content. Good writing is lean. It moves easily and smoothly.

Wordiness is often caused by simple repetition, as in this selection from a student paper:

> My primary aim in life is to improve myself. The way I hope to accomplish this aim is by receiving a college education, for a college education gives a person the opportunity by which he can improve himself. The tools that one receives in college are essential to a person who wants to improve himself.

By eliminating the obvious repetitions we can compress this to:

> My primary aim in life is to improve myself. I hope to accomplish this by acquiring the essential tools for achievement through a college education.

This passage is still vague, since it lacks any specific delineation of what the writer means by "achievement" and "essential tools." But as a generalized introduction it might justify its twenty-five words. The original, though, was fifty-five words, over twice as long, yet said no more.

The stylistic faults we've discussed—pomposity, vagueness, inaccuracy, and wordiness—have been singled out because they're the most common deterrents to the development of an effective style, one that is *clear* and *compressed*. After some of your papers have been commented upon by an instructor, though, you should be able to identify your own most common faults. Almost all writers exhibit certain recurring tendencies. Some are always wordy, while others are vague, pompous, or careless in their use of words. By analyzing your instructor's comments you can find out where you should concentrate your efforts. If you discover that your papers are consistently vague, for instance, pay particular attention to the use of concrete examples when going over your rough draft.

Naturally there are many more characteristics than those we have mentioned—both good and bad —that contribute to the quality of a piece of writing. Clarity and compression are not the only virtues, and the weaknesses cited above are not the only flaws. Much has to be mastered in the pursuit of excellence in writing, as in anything else.

But a style that is both clear and compressed is also precise, specific, direct, natural, and well-paced. If your writing possesses all these qualities it will serve you well on the vast majority of occasions.

Mechanics

You should now be ready to put the final touches on your manuscript before recopying it as your final draft. Up to this point we've concentrated on matters of content and style, postponing the work on mechanics—punctuation, spelling, and grammar—until the paper has assumed its final shape. Even if you produce several intermediate drafts in revising content and style, as you might for an important assignment, you should still leave the mechanics until everything else has been done.

Mechanics and Style

Much of the trouble students have with one major aspect of mechanics—sentence structure—is closely related to the stylistic problems discussed in the preceding section. A student who writes pompously, vaguely, wordily, or inaccurately is much more likely to commit serious blunders in sentence structure than one who states his ideas directly and naturally.

One of the best ways to improve your mechanics, therefore, is through the development of a clear and concise style.

What You Know, and Don't Know

Students probably worry more about correctness than anything else. Yet mechanical problems are not that significant for most college students. Some of course do have serious deficiencies, but students usually know a great deal more about mechanics than they imagine. Their difficulties are typically very few, and very specific. Even students who make a great many errors often simply make the same mistakes over and over.

As noted earlier, you've developed language skills not so much from school as from the natural process of everyday learning. In your speech you've learned to express your thoughts within the basic grammatical structure of the language through the continuing process of listening and speaking and reading, often without being consciously aware of the knowledge you're absorbing.

The mechanics of writing do not represent a new and different body of knowledge which has to be mastered from scratch. These conventions are simply a more codified version of language patterns you have already learned to employ in speech.

Still you may have been told so often that you "don't know grammar" that you are convinced you still have to master an enormous body of complex material in order to eliminate your errors.

This is rarely true. If you have problems in this area, you can effectively remedy them in three practical steps:

Identifying Your Problems. It's surprising how many students whose papers are graded down for mechanical flaws are unable to say just what their problems are. Your first step, then, is to replace any generalized feeling of inadequacy with a precise awareness of what you're doing wrong.

Do this by analyzing the comments instructors have made on your papers and by composing a list of your most common mistakes. You can do this in conjunction with a survey of your papers for stylistic flaws, as suggested in the preceding section. In general, you'll find an even more clearly defined pattern of mistakes in mechanics, with the same faults occurring again and again. In other words, you'll probably find that you've done most things right and that relatively few *kinds* of mistakes account for most of the red marks.

Concentrating on Your Weaknesses. Rather than attempting a vague program of general improvement, attack your specific problems one by one. You can begin by consulting a handbook that treats mechanics in a clear and practical manner. If you don't own such a book, ask your instructor for a recommendation. Study the sections that deal with your identified problems. If this doesn't help, try another book that may explain the material better. You can also request help from an instructor, a campus writing clinic, or a more advanced student.

Spelling should be treated as a special case. If you're a poor speller, there's not much a handbook or an instructor can do to help. You have to work on your own. Keep a list of every word you misspell, not only in your English papers but in all your work, adding to it as you go along and memorizing the correct spelling of each word. Go over the whole list at regular intervals, making sure you know how to spell every word on it.

Of the thousands of words you know and use, only a relatively few will give you trouble. By focusing on these, you can produce a dramatic improvement in a short time.

Guarding against Your Faults. In reworking your rough draft, look *specifically* for the kinds of mistakes you tend to make. Many students have trouble eliminating mechanical errors because they're not really looking for them. They merely read aimlessly through the paper to make sure "it looks all right." By trying to see everything at once they often fail to see anything at all.

Work directly from the list of your most common errors. If you've generally had trouble with spelling, sentence fragments, and pronoun reference, for example, search actively for these three kinds of faults. Go through the rough draft once, looking only for spelling errors and checking particularly words that you've misspelled before. Then look just for sentence fragments, and then for faulty pronoun references.

As simple as it sounds, these three steps can be remarkably successful in eliminating the problems causing you the most trouble. You will still of course want to check your rough draft for other mechanical mistakes. But your main emphasis should be on the clearly identified errors you are likeliest to commit.

As a practical aid in looking for mechanical mistakes, you may want to try an unusual but efficient technique employed by some newspaper reporters. Since deadlines give them little time for revision, they read their work *backward*—not from the last word to the first, but from the last *sentence* to the first. Each sentence is read in its normal phrasing, just as it is written. But the last sentence of the story is read first, and then the next to last, and so on, back to the first.

Although this technique obviously works only for mechanical errors and some of the more self-contained stylistic flaws, such as inaccurate word usage, it allows you to discover these flaws by concentrating on each sentence as an independent unit, without being carried along by the narrative flow of the paper.

You should type or write your final draft only after you are satisfied that you have successfully completed the work of planning and revising. In some cases, you may write one or more intermediate drafts before producing one that you are ready to turn in.

All work that you submit should be carefully proofread in its final form. This takes only a few minutes in most cases but can significantly improve the overall quality of your paper through the correction of careless and often obvious mistakes or omissions.

Considering Your Audience

If you were a professional writer asked to do an article on the future of space exploration, your first question would be a simple one: Who's it for? You would obviously handle the subject differently for

Scientific American than you would for *Boy's Life*, *Reader's Digest*, or *Playboy*.

Should you, for instance, explain what the Van Allen radiation belt is, or can you expect your readers to be knowledgeable about atmospheric physics? Can you assume your readers are interested in space travel, or will you have to gain their attention with a lively beginning and hold it throughout with anecdotes, stories, humorous interludes, and human interest sidelights? Should your discussion emphasize the adventure and drama of space flights, the technical aspects, the scientific potential, or the economic, political, and social implications?

Even your style will be influenced by the readers you hope to attract. Should your sentences and paragraphs be short and simple and your vocabulary easily understood, or should you treat the subject in a complex, detailed, sophisticated manner? Should your tone be personal and casual, or will your readers expect formal restraint and scientific objectivity?

Many instructors inform you whom you should be writing for, often suggesting that the class be your audience. In that case, words and concepts familiar to the average college student do not have to be explained, but specialized terms do. If you're not clear about your intended audience, you should ask the instructor for guidance.

For most college writing, you need only know enough to decide

1. How formal or informal your tone and usage should be
2. What background your audience possesses

Unless otherwise instructed, you would probably do best maintaining a *middle-ground* approach. In other words,

1. Your tone, vocabulary, and phrasing should fall within the broad outlines of *standard English*, avoiding both an overuse of slang and an excessive dependence on obscure words and "elevated" phrasing.
2. You should assume an audience of intelligence and education, with good general knowledge but little background in specialized fields.

The concept of *appropriateness* should guide you in responding to a particular writing assignment. Your handling should be appropriate to the subject, to your purpose, to your background, and to the characteristics of your audience. In general, you should respond sensibly to the overall *situation*, just as you do almost automatically in social situations.

WRITING EXPOSITION: SOME FINAL WORDS

The time you spend on a paper, from preliminary notes to final draft, will of course vary a great deal. Some writers can produce a relatively "clean" first draft which needs little revision. Others need a great deal of rethinking and rewriting.

The pattern we've suggested will allow you to work in an organized fashion under a wide variety of conditions, as it can be condensed or expanded as you see fit. It cannot of course guarantee an excellent paper. The quality of your writing will largely be determined by your intelligence, your effort, and the overall language facility you've attained during the course of your life, both in school and out. Writing is a skill that must be acquired gradually and through practice.

The pattern we've suggested can help you write up to your capacity by enabling you to make the most of the skills you do possess, to eliminate your major difficulties, and to further develop your ability as you continue to write.

Chapter 7

Evaluating What You Read: Persuasive Writing

Most of us are convinced that we're coolly rational persons who examine evidence impartially and arrive at clear-cut, inevitable conclusions. The truth is that we're rarely aware of the process by which we reach decisions. Logic and evidence surely play a part. But so do emotion, faith, prejudices, uninformed attitudes, wishful thinking, misinformation, false pride, fear, insecurity and ignorance. In this chapter you'll learn some of the ways writers can manipulate these powerful nonrational forces, and some of the ways you can protect yourself against such manipulations.

Without too much oversimplification, we can say that all our attitudes toward most matters, large and small, are in some way the product of *logic*, *emotion*, or *faith*, usually is some combination. It's often difficult of course to say which is predominant, or in what proportions they are intermingled. Do we vote for a presidential candidate because we have logically examined the issues and evaluated his competence? Because we feel in some way emotionally reassured by his appearance and manner? Or because we have faith in the principles of the party or the political theory he represents?

Each of these three methods of arriving at conclusions is valid, and there is little point in trying to untangle the intricate relationships between them every time we make up our minds about something. What can be valuable, though, is to learn enough about the way we make decisions to keep others from controlling this process for their own benefit. Your goal is to become as skillful in evaluating the methods employed by writers—and others—to influence your opinions and your behaviors, as these people are in using such methods.

The Critical Reader

To be a critical reader doesn't mean simply to find fault. It means to weigh, judge, and evaluate. A critical reader can distinguish a fact from an opinion, a proof from an assertion, and a legitimate argument from a false appeal.

He is also sensitive to the use and misuse of words. He pays attention to the writer's tone and emphasis and scrutinizes the role that sarcasm, ridicule, humor, and satire can play in making a point. He is aware of suggestions, implications, and disguised conclusions. He distrusts easy solutions to hard problems and superficial discussions of complex subjects. He hates being fooled, tricked, or misled and refuses to accept anything without good cause. Finally, he does not assume that everything he sees in print is true or that every writer's motives are above suspicion.

In the preceding chapters dealing with pure exposition, we noted that such purity of type is unusual. As we will now see, the author whose main purpose is to inform usually, in addition, tries to persuade you to accept both his information and the conclusions derived from it. Conversely, the writer whose main purpose is to persuade almost always informs you about certain matters while doing so.

Persuasive writing, then, should always be considered *exposition plus persuasion*. And your objective should no longer be merely to understand, but to *understand* and to *evaluate*.

UNDERSTANDING PERSUASIVE WRITING

In working toward an understanding of persuasive writing, you should follow *the basic reading pattern for exposition* explained in earlier chapters. In addition, you should seek full comprehension of the two basic elements of persuasive writing, the author's *techniques of persuasion* and his *conclusions*.

The writer's techniques of persuasion are the means by which he hopes to convince you to accept his conclusions. They may or may not be legitimate. The writer's conclusions are the opinions or attitudes he wants you to accept, which may or may not be supported by convincing evidence.

You'll normally find these persuasive elements closely allied with the basic expository elements. For instance, a writer's main point (in exposition) is generally the same as his conclusion (in persuasion). You'll also find an obvious relationship between the organization of his exposition and his techniques of persuasion.

Your understanding of a persuasive writer's techniques and conclusions should gradually improve as you progress through the three steps of the basic reading pattern, just as your understanding of the expository elements improves. From the rather generalized impressions of the preliminary survey, you should proceed to the full and detailed comprehension of your final recapitulation.

EVALUATING PERSUASIVE TECHNIQUES

Generally, you should first evaluate a writer's techniques and then his conclusions. If the writer's techniques are not legitimate, the unprepared reader may find himself tricked into accepting conclusions he would otherwise reject.

We won't attempt to draw fine distinctions between categories, and will disregard both the rigorous discipline of formal logic and the Latin terminology that often accompanies it. Our only purpose is to acquaint you with the more popular devices of faulty persuasion and to illustrate their common reliance on unjustifiable appeals.

Faulty Techniques of Persuasion

We'll group these illegitimate techniques under three categories, according to their dependence on *irrelevant emotions*, *incomplete presentation*, or *illogical thinking*.

Irrelevant Emotions

When a writer tries to arouse and control your emotions without your knowledge, and when these emotions are not relevant, then his attempts at persuasion should be questioned.

Transfer. A writer often tries to make you transfer to the situation at hand certain emotions previously formed about something else:

> The Republican party is the party of Lincoln.
> The Democratic party is the party of Jefferson.

In advertising, the similar use of a public figure produces a *testimonial advertisement*, wherein a popular sports or entertainment figure, for instance, is linked with the use of a product in the hope that people will transfer their approval of the person to the object being advertised.

The same technique can be used in reverse, urging you to reject something by giving it unfavorable connections (*name-calling*):

> My opponent's ideas sound just like those spouted by the Communists (or Fascists, radicals, hippies, bigots, etc.).

As with all persuasive devices, the transfer is most effective when handled subtlely. Glance, for instance, through a popular magazine to see how skillfully advertisers create a pleasing visual context for their products—beautiful and happy people against backdrops of verdant meadows and fresh mountain streams.

Although we're primarily concerned with verbal communication, visual effects are commonly employed in conjunction with written presentations. A newspaper editor, for example, may each day receive a dozen or more photographs of the president. He may publish the most, or the least, flattering. If the policy of the paper dictates it, he may consistently use favorable or unfavorable photographs without the readers ever realizing that such a prejudicial selection process is going on.

Direct Emotional Appeals. The often subtle efforts to make you transfer feelings frequently give way to more direct appeals to your emotions. A writer can, for instance, *flatter* you—but only if you agree with him:

> Certainly all intelligent and responsible patriots will accept these ideas.

He can try to arouse your *fear* of doing the wrong thing:

> Only the stupid and irresponsible could fail to agree with my program.

He can *ridicule* opposing ideas, or the people who support them, implying that you would become ridiculous yourself if you accepted them:

> That idea sounds like something a ten-year-old boy would come up with if his allowance were cut off.

He can arouse your *pity*:

> Surely a widowed woman with three children to support deserves your vote for the state senate.

Similarly, a writer can sway you by arousing your feelings of hatred, shame, disgust, love, sympathy, etc.

The almost universal desire to conform to accepted standards of thought and behavior forms the basis of the *bandwagon* technique. The writer tries to convince you that everybody is doing something, or believing something, and that you'd better jump on the bandwagon before it's too late.

> All your friends and neighbors are supporting this program.
> This is the style people are wearing this spring.

The writer may also attempt to *bully* the reader into accepting or rejecting an idea:

> Naturally, you can see the undeniable logic of this idea.
> I'm sure no one here is foolish enough to suggest that....

When a writer arouses your fears, your egotism, your insecurities, or your desire to conform, make sure that a legitimate basis exists for such emotional responses. If there is none, the emotion is irrelevant and should be discounted.

Incomplete Presentation

You should be cautious in accepting a writer's conclusions when they are obviously based on a fragmentary or incomplete presentation.

Faulty Generalizations. The careless use of such words as "all," "always," "never," "no one," and "everybody" is a sign of incomplete presentation when these broad generalizations are not justified by the evidence presented:

> Deficit spending, by governments or individuals, always leads to economic ruin.

Sometimes the generalizing word is merely suggested:

> A student who does poorly in high school will do just as poorly in college.

"Always" is clearly implied here. Unless the writer supports this sweeping generalization, the statement needs to be qualified with "sometimes," "often," "usually," or some other limiting word.

Oversimplification. A writer often oversimplifies a complex situation in order to persuade you to accept his conclusions:

> Strikes should be outlawed, for they cause inconvenience to innocent people.

Vagueness. A writer can also oversimplify by using abstract terms which he does not define:

> Teenagers are responsible for the majority of serious automobile accidents.

Without a concrete definition of "serious," this sentence remains vague and meaningless.

Card-Stacking. Many writers stack the cards in their own favor by giving you only one side—theirs—of an issue. Even though an author's arguments seem convincing, you must remember that equally convincing arguments could possibly be found on the other side.

Illogical Thinking

A writer may try to win over his reader by *pretending* to use logical proofs. He may benefit from a superficial appearance of logic, while shying away from the real thing, in several ways:

Begging the Question. Someone "begs the question" when his statement is so worded as to be self-proving:

> Anyone who works at it hard enough can become a successful businessman.

It's impossible to disprove this statement. If you cite examples of hard workers who failed in business, the writer can say they didn't work "hard enough."

Confusing Fact and Opinion. In presenting an argument, a writer normally uses both facts and opinions. If honest, he will clearly distinguish between them. If he fails to do so, you must decide for yourself which is which:

> Students receive a better education at a small college than at a large university.
>
> The most important prerequisite for a presidential candidate is a knowledge of international affairs.
>
> Thomas Mann is the greatest novelist of the twentieth century.

You may or may not agree with the above opinions. But you should realize they *are* opinions, and nothing more.

Unproved Assumptions. When a writer bases his proof on a statement that needs proving itself (and that may be an opinion masquerading as fact), his conclusions are immediately suspect:

> Since the lack of recreational facilities is the main cause of juvenile delinquency, we can then say that . . . .

The basic assumption may also be so vague and inexact as to be meaningless:

> Trouble in the home is caused by a clash of personalities. Therefore . . . .

False Cause and Effect. Sometimes a writer claims a cause-and-effect relationship between certain events when this relationship may be merely coincidental:

> The same year Baxter became mayor, traffic accidents in our city increased fifteen percent. We need a mayor who will be more safety conscious.

False Analogy. An *analogy* is a comparison that stresses similarities. A writer using an analogy implies that the matter under discussion is similar enough to something else to be considered in the same way:

> If democracy can work in the country, it can work in the classroom.
>
> The army depends on obedience to authority, and a school does too.

In examining an analogy, you should be especially wary of oversimplification and the careless transfer of emotions.

Distortion. Through oversight or dishonesty, a writer may distort his material so as to give a false or misleading picture. He can do this in so many ways that it would be difficult to categorize them. A writer may, for instance, present false information. Or he may, as in card-stacking, select facts in such a way as to produce a biased effect.

One form of distortion is based on the use of *misleading statistics*. This often occurs in advertising, and perhaps it would be worthwhile to look at the following hypothetical example in some detail:

> Three out of four dentists polled said they recommend brand X toothpaste for their patients.

Even conceding that the figure "three out of four" is accurate, our first question might deal with the extensiveness of the poll. Were only four dentists questioned? Four hundred? Four thousand? Were the dentists preselected on the basis of a particular bias or predisposition? Was it a local, regional, or national sampling? Who took the poll? Was it the only one taken, or were numerous trial polls commissioned and only the most "successful" one cited in the advertisement?

Although the advertisement does not claim that three out of four dentists *in the country* recommend their brand, this is what the advertisers are clearly implying and want the reader to believe. The advertisement further implies that the dentists in question recommend *only* this brand, or at least recommend it *over* competing brands. But it's possible that the dentists simply recommended brand-X *along with* several other brands which they considered more or less equal. It's even possible that brand X, although recommended, had *less* support than some other brands.

Needless to say, it's not fair to put the worst possible interpretation upon every statement. But nothing in the advertisement prevents us from assuming the worst, and common sense suggests that, since the advertiser has a vested interest in selling his product, his presentation of statistical evidence ought to be viewed with some skepticism.

The use of visual techniques should again be mentioned, since a good deal of statistical manipulation can occur in the use of graphs, charts, and illustrations. A few examples can show how even very simple presentations can distort the facts.

Let's assume that the operating expenses of a university have risen in a year's time from $50 million to $60 million. There are several ways this information can be portrayed graphically. If we wish to emphasize the magnitude of the increase, we can place it on a graph like the one in Figure 7-1.

If we want to make the increase appear less significant, we can flatten out the upward curve by extending the line as shown in Figure 7-2.

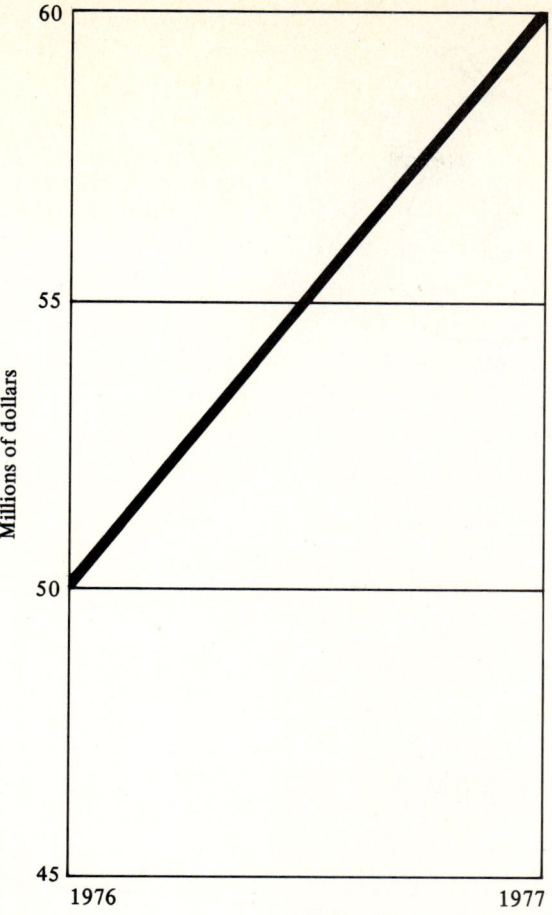

Figure 7-1

Figure 7-3 indicates other ways of making it seem larger.

And the treatments shown in Figure 7-4 make it seem smaller.

In none of these cases are the facts altered. The distortion occurs only through the impression created by the various forms of presentation. Yet each of these graphic displays, taken by itself, has the appearance of statistical objectivity.

As noted, these are rather obvious examples. Nothing short of becoming a statistician can prepare you to evaluate the sophisticated use of statistical data. As an intelligent reader, however, you can at least be aware of the potential for misrepresentation and not allow the mere appearance of scientific "factuality" to overawe you.

Perhaps it would be helpful to establish for yourself a manageable set of guidelines which will allow you to approach persuasive writing intelligently. We have divided the various faulty techniques into three categories:

1. Appeals to irrelevant emotions
2. Incomplete presentation
3. Illogical thinking

You may find it easier to remember the various techniques of faulty persuasion by noting that they usually occur whenever a writer

1. Brings in material that doesn't belong
2. Leaves out material that does belong
3. Distorts the material he presents

Slanted Writing

What we have been dealing with in this chapter can be simply classified as *slanted writing*, in which the author slants his presentation in order to persuade the reader. He may use any of the techniques we've listed, and many more besides.

In our discussion of *connotation*, we noted the different shadings of words with similar meanings. Thus a writer suggests quite different things when characterizing a person as shrewd, wise, knowing, cunning, wily, slick, or sagacious. And readers react to these implications, often without being aware of it.

Read, for instance, these two brief passages about contemporary political figures. In both cases

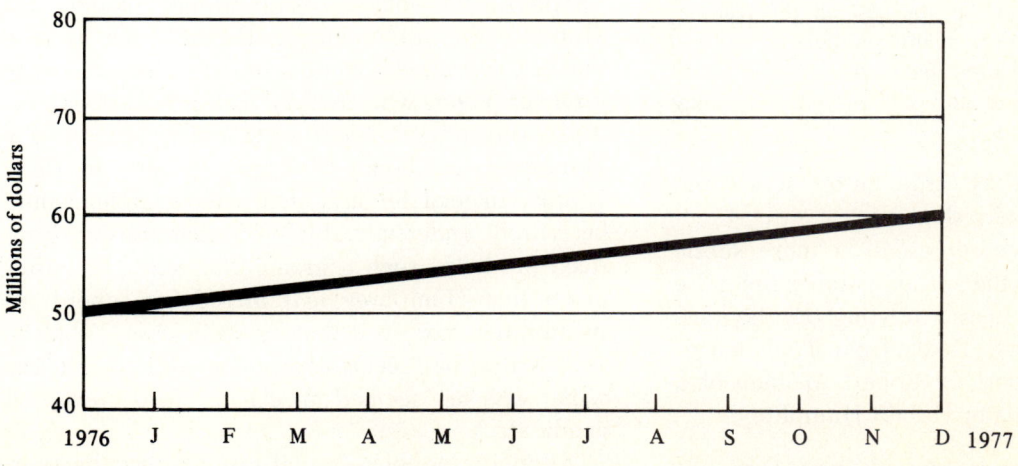

Figure 7-2

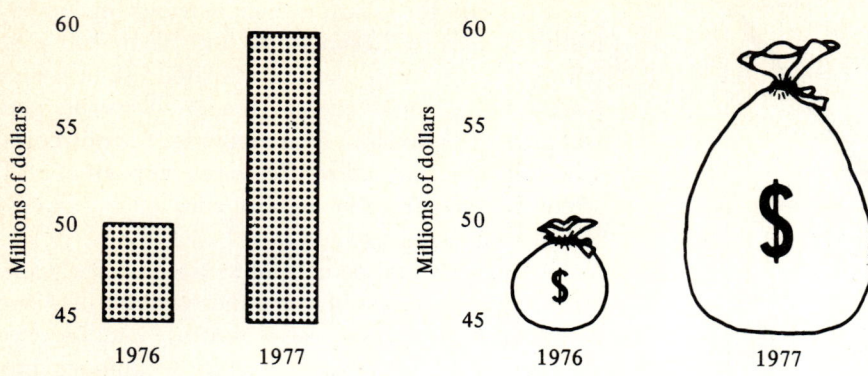

Figure 7-3

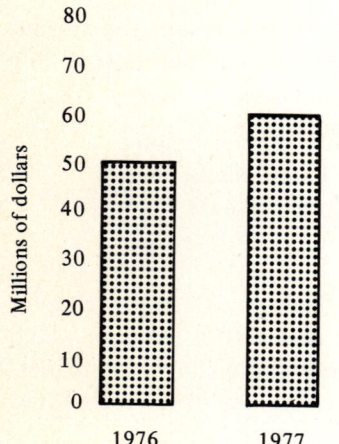
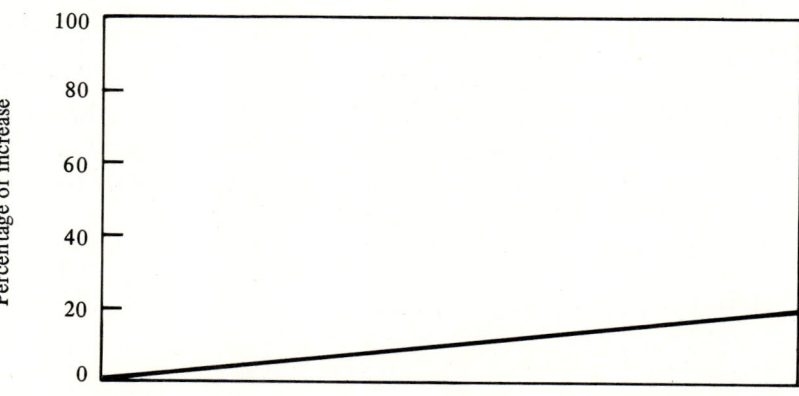

Figure 7-4

the writer wished to foster a negative impression. The first excerpt, from a column by Tom Wicker in the *New York Times*, can be cited as an example of *name-calling*:

> George Wallace has lapsed for the first time in years into his true gutter style. At a news conference in Montgomery the other day, he cast off the respectable robes in which too many politicians and too much of the national press have tried to drape him and came out snarling and kicking like the alley fighter he is.

Obviously such terms as "true gutter style" and "alley fighter" are heavily slanted.

The second instance represents a more subtle form of slanting, since the author assumes the guise of an observer who is merely relating the thoughts and reactions of others. Taken from *Time* magazine, it's part of a report by Robert Ajemian of a visit to the home of Senator Hubert Humphrey:

> "People are happy to see me wherever I go," he says. "I've never had it this way before." He seems almost incredulous as he adds: "They ask me to run."
> If that prospect brings a groan from voters who are tired of windy old Hubert, it's surely understandable. Even by 1968, Humphrey seemed an exhausted, overexposed candidate, a veritable Swiss cheese of political wounds.

Despite some obvious name-calling ("windy old Hubert") the author implies that it is not he who makes this characterization, but rather some vague group of "*voters* who are tired of windy old Hubert." The writer doesn't even say that the prospect of a Humphrey candidacy "brings a groan" to these people. Instead he says that such a groan would be "surely understandable"—"*if* that prospect" indeed produced such a groan. Nor does the writer claim that Humphrey *was* incredulous about his possibilities, nor even that he *seemed* so. What he says is that he "seems *almost* incredulous." In the same way, he "*seemed* an exhausted, overexposed candidate."

Although less of a frontal assault than the comments about Wallace, this passage too is easy to spot as slanted writing when it is isolated and subjected to even a superficial scrutiny. The problem for many readers is that they fail to remain alert to the possibility that writing *might* be slanted. They accept slanting so casually that they're not aware of how common it is and how significantly it affects their responses.

At this point you may wonder if any legitimate means of persuasion exist. Naturally they do. The techniques we've discussed are faulty because they do not, in themselves, legitimately support a conclusion. They represent the avoidance of a true argument, since their effectiveness is based on appearance rather than reality. Thus the term "fallacy" means more than something that is simply false. A fallacy is something that is false even though it *appears* to be true. All these techniques, it should be emphasized, exist unto themselves, apart from whatever subject is being discussed. They can be made to fit any subject.

To analyze a writer's arguments, then, you should judge his techniques without reference to his subject or his general attitudes, and without being influenced by your own preconceptions about the writer or subject. Because you agree with someone doesn't mean his techniques are valid. Nor, if you disagree, does it mean his techniques are faulty.

Distinguishing Good Techniques from Bad Ones

Means of persuasion can be considered acceptable if the support they present is (1) relevant, (2) complete, and (3) logical.

In other words, does the writer keep out material that doesn't belong, bring in everything that does belong, and refrain from distorting his material? He should be honest and aboveboard in his emotional appeals and should present the issues fairly and fully. He should develop his arguments logically, without resorting to false or confused reasoning. Finally, he should admit to his own biases and take reasonable care to distinguish facts from opinions.

Once you have evaluated the writer's *means* of persuasion, you can proceed to the equally important step of evaluating his *conclusions*.

EVALUATING A WRITER'S CONCLUSIONS

Because a writer's conclusions can be various without limit, touching every conceivable area of knowledge, no single approach will be consistently effective in evaluating them. Your success will always rest primarily on your ability as a *critical reader*—on your intelligence and alertness. However, in evaluating the writer's conclusions you can be guided by the answers to these questions:

1. Can the writer's *means* be considered partially or completely *faulty*? Of course, you must remember that faulty means do not *necessarily* lead to a faulty conclusion. A conclusion is not always wrong because one writer fails to support it adequately.
2. Can the writer's *means* be considered partially or completely *acceptable*? The conclusions a writer develops from acceptable means normally prove to be valid. But you must always beware of the fallacy—the *apparently* legitimate argument—and of the legitimate argument somehow twisted to support illegitimate conclusions.
3. Are there any *implied or unstated conclusions* which must be evaluated? Such implied conclusions are often simply *attitudes* a writer wishes you to accept, and you should make an attempt to identify these attitudes and subject them to the same scrutiny as the conclusions that are directly stated.
4. Does the author, by use of acceptable means, *prove* any or all of his conclusions? Again, however, you must beware of proofs that only appear to be valid. Absolute proof demands the impartial presentation of incontrovertible evidence.
5. Do the conclusions *not* proved lend themselves to proof? In broader, more abstract areas of life and thought, final proof is difficult or impossible to attain. If factual proof isn't possible, the writer should not *pretend* to give it. By the same token, you should not expect to receive it.
6. Have you made fair allowance for your own *prejudices* and *preconceived opinions*? Justice Holmes once observed that, "To doubt one's own basic assumptions is the mark of a civilized man." You have been learning to doubt and criticize the ideas of others. But to be a truly intelligent reader you must also doubt your own.

To read persuasive writing with an inflexible mind is a waste of time. An intelligent reader listens to arguments so that he may, if the situation warrants, accept new ideas or modify old ones. Aware of his limited knowledge in most fields, he remains open-minded but cautious and tries to hear presentations on both sides before committing himself.

EXERCISES

1. Study carefully and then evaluate the following examples of persuasive writing. In each case, determine the writer's major conclusion, even if it is only implied. Are the means used to support

the conclusion legitimate? If not, in what manner do they fall short? Find the specific words and sentences that weaken the presentation. Are the conclusions valid? If not, why not? In which cases would you reject the conclusions, and in which would you merely withhold judgment? What unstated attitudes, if any, are the writers trying to make you accept?

a. A letter to the editor of the *New York Times,* discussing the admission policies at the City University of New York:

> An odd premise appears to figure in the current arguments in favor of retaining Open Admissions at C.U.N.Y. It is that since students who are unable to meet the proposed entrance requirements are not to blame for their inability, they deserve to be let in; they should not be penalized because it is not their fault that they cannot read.
>
> But this is surely nonsense. A puny man may not be to blame for his physique, but it hardly follows that he deserves a spot on the Jets' squad. The issue of blameworthiness must be distinguished from that of deficiency. That a student ought not to be blamed for his reading deficiency does not mean that he can read.
>
> It is reasonable to hold that reading ability beyond the eighth-grade level is necessary for academic success. A student without this and other qualifications is unlikely to profit from attendance at a university (individual success stories notwithstanding), and the university community is unlikely to profit from his presence.
>
> To view rejection from a university as an (undeserved) penalty is to view acceptance at a university as a right. This it certainly is not. One has a right to apply. Acceptance is, and ought to be, an independent matter.

b. A letter to the editor of the *Arizona Daily Star* (Tucson):

> There is a bill proposed in Arizona which would require the registration of firearms. Individuals of good repute are working for this bill. I wonder if they realize what they are backing?
>
> Expertness in the use of small arms is an American heritage. It is this knowledge of firearms, which together with courage, has won battles from Bunker Hill and the Alamo to the mountains of Korea. A man in Soviet Russia cannot own an arm without a permit from the police and registration. The same thing happened in Axis Germany. It must not happen here.

c. A brief excerpt from a student paper:

> Our country has been, is, and will continue to be a refuge for the unfortunate. That is a simple fact no one can deny.

d. The opening paragraphs of a nationally syndicated column by Andrew M. Greeley:

> Busing and gun control represent the same phenomenon in American life—a tiny, well-organized and affluent minority are able to impose their will on the rest of the country because politicians are afraid to offend those minorities.
>
> The National Rifle Association with its sophisticated lobbyists, its morally self-righteous members, and its potent campaign chest is able to block effective gun control even though the vast majority of Americans want it. There are, one suspects, very few Congressmen who are not worried sick about the large number of guns on the loose in the country; but they are even more worried about what the NRA can do if it aims its sights at them.
>
> The "civil rights" lobby—made up of liberal intellectuals (most of them white) whose children go to private schools—is able to force busing on the nation, even though the majority of white and black parents reject it and only a very small group of either race list it as their preferred means of racial integration. But again, moral fervor, organization, and financial clout scare the living daylights out of the plastic liberals who are seeking the Democratic nomination.

e. A letter to the editor of the *Springfield* (Massachusetts) *Daily News*:

> While liberal eggheads and left-wing fellow-travelers focus their petty scorn on the activities of our beleaugered CIA, America is steadily creeping towards a fate so diabolically subtle as to conceal its disastrously evil implications. I am referring to the impending conversion to the metric system. This seemingly harmless conversion amounts to a subversion of the United States.
>
> Why should America switch to the metric system in the first place? Without it, we became the world's number 1 power; with the partial use of metrics in recent years, our youth has begun to question basic American values, and our nation has lost its security against Red aggression.
>
> The metric system is un-American. It was developed in France during the 1790's—a product of their bloody, anarchistic and godless revolution! . . . How can law abiding, God-fearing Americans adopt something so alien to our national heritage?
>
> Think of the chaos that will result if we switch to this alien, socialistic system of weights and measures! How many of you know how to calculate in hectares, kiloliters or dekagrams? One can well imagine the confusion and disorganization our armed forces would suffer during such a transition period.
>
> What a golden opportunity for the zealous disciples of Lenin and Stalin to take advantage

of a dis-oriented America in the throes of metrification!

There is nothing wrong with the American system of weights and measures, and there is no reason why we shouldn't insist that the rest of the world adopt it. Such a proposal would find its most vehement opponents within the Communist bloc, for it would thwart their grand designs for world domination

I suppose we'll soon replace the American dollar with the Russian ruble!

2. Read and evaluate several editorials or political columns in a local paper.
3. Read and evaluate several *news stories* (including the headlines) on controversial subjects in a local paper. Are the stories examples of impartial exposition, as good reporting is supposed to be? Is there any evidence of an attempt to persuade you to accept certain conclusions? Is the writing slanted in any way? Are the means of persuasion obvious or disguised? Are they legitimate? Would the average reader be aware of their presence?
4. Read and evaluate a complete article (including the title and subtitles) about a controversial public figure in a popular magazine. Is the writer trying to persuade you to accept a certain attitude about this person? How does he go about doing so? Is his conclusion stated or implied?
5. Analyze the photographs accompanying the above-mentioned article. Do they appear to have been selected to show the subject in a noticeably favorable or unfavorable light? Do the captions show any evidence of slanted writing? If there seems to be a bias in the photographs and captions, does it correspond to the bias you found in the article itself?
6. Over the next few weeks or so, pay particular attention to the photographs of your governor or mayor or some other prominent figure as they appear in your local newspaper. Or do the same for the president or another well-known national figure in *Time* or *Newsweek*. Can you discern any pattern of either positive or negative bias in the photographs published?

Chapter 8

Writing Persuasion

The pattern used for writing exposition (Chapter 6) can also serve as the basis for writing persuasion. Beyond that, your goal as a writer of persuasion is to develop a forceful but legitimate presentation of your views. Your approach should be marked by a sense of fairness and responsibility and by a determination to treat your material honestly.

As a check on yourself, you should devote a portion of the time spent revising your rough draft to a consideration of your *persuasive techniques*, concentrating on them just as you do on *content*, *style*, and *mechanics*. You may find it helpful to resurvey the preceding chapter before doing this.

Based on what you've learned, note the deficiencies in the following sentence from a student paper:

> Since the laws of the Bible are in all cases for the betterment of society and the individual, it is definitely necessary that people of all ages, and especially teenagers, support their country's rules and laws.

It begins with an unproved assumption ("Since the laws of the Bible are . . .") which is really an opinion disguised as a fact, fails to allow for even a single exception ("in *all* cases"), and leans heavily on an undefined abstraction ("the betterment of society and the individual"). It bullies the reader ("it is definitely necessary"), makes unsupported claims ("people of all ages, and especially teenagers"), and concludes by turning the whole sentence into a false analogy.

This is an extreme example, and of course it's always easier to find weaknesses in someone else's writing than in your own. In polishing your first draft, though, you should make a real effort to evaluate your persuasive techniques as objectively as possible.

It's especially important to remember that your techniques may be faulty even though your opinions are valid. Students often defend their work by saying, "But that's what I believe." This doesn't, however, justify careless or inadequate presentation.

In many cases, you can improve your argument by simply toning down some of your assertions, since a common problem in student writing is that of *overstating* ideas which, if phrased more moderately, might be perfectly acceptable:

There's no question but that everyone who participates in ROTC gains a lot from the experience.

The same point could be better made with restraint:

Most of the men who participate in ROTC gain a lot from the experience.

Success in persuasive writing always depends to a large extent upon the *reasonableness* with which you present your case.

TWO TYPES OF PERSUASIVE WRITING

Assignments in persuasive writing generally fall into two categories. The distinction between them isn't always made clear in the assignment, so it's often up to you to determine which kind is called for and to respond accordingly. One asks you to set forth a *factual presentation* that leads to a logical conclusion. The other asks you to express your *personal opinions*.

The Factual Presentation

This assignment requires you to act as an impartial investigator. It assumes that you will begin without preconceived attitudes toward the subject, or that you will put aside any you may have.

The following topics are typical of those usually considered appropriate for a factual presentation:

Alcohol and traffic accidents
Sentencing procedures in juvenile court
High school dress and grooming codes
Local rent control and university housing
Air power in the European War, 1939–1941
Business support of the arts: A case study
Violence on television
The seniority system in Congress
Pesticides and cotton farming
The open classroom
State House lobbying
The education program in a county jail
Student participation in campus government
University support of women's athletics

Many of these topics could also be treated as *pure exposition* in which the facts would be presented for the sole purpose of informing the reader. If you're instructed, however, to evaluate the facts and draw a conclusion from them, you're being asked to write a persuasive paper.

This doesn't mean that you must, at all costs, convince the reader to accept your conclusions. There's no reason to consider the paper a battleground, with you and your reader locked in combat. A persuasive assignment simply requires you to offer reasonable support for a particular point of view. You can go about doing this by carrying out the following steps:

1. Gathering information
2. Forming a conclusion
3. Presenting the facts and the conclusion in a credible manner

Your success will be determined by the thoroughness with which you gather information, the intelligence with which you arrive at a conclusion, and the effectiveness with which you present and support this conclusion.

Gathering Information

A factual presentation usually requires research. It may be a modest amount for a short paper, or a great deal for a long one. In either case, you will be expected to seek the facts objectively and to withhold judgment until you have gained enough knowledge to make a fair evaluation of the subject. You'll probably want to concentrate on gathering factual material but should not ignore the opinions and conclusions of authorities in the field, especially when they seem well supported.

The form and quantity of your research notes will naturally be determined by the assignment. For a formal paper requiring footnotes and a bibliography, you'll obviously need extensive notes. [For a discussion of the use of the library, research techniques, note taking, etc., you can refer to Elinor Yaggy, *How to Write Your Term Paper* (New York: Thomas Y. Crowell, 1974).]

Forming a Conclusion

Several different conclusions could of course be reached for each of the topics listed above. Few of these subjects lend themselves to absolute scientific objectivity, and two intelligent and fair-minded persons could understandably arrive at opposite positions. This is particularly true of a topic like "violence on television." A great deal of research has been undertaken, but the experts frequently disagree with one another, and the facts themselves are often in dispute, since the results of many of the studies seem to be contradictory.

That shouldn't frighten you away from this or similarly controversial subjects. You're not expected, after all, to arrive at the "right" answer. In many cases there's no such thing. Nor would conscientious instructors penalize you for a conclusion they disagree with. What your instructors expect is that you will arrive at a reasonable conclusion that represents a rational, but human, response to the facts.

Presenting Facts and a Conclusion in a Credible Manner

Up to this point the work has been largely preparatory. You've done the research and evaluation and arrived at a conclusion. Now you're ready to begin writing.

As you proceed, you may discover that gaps exist in your knowledge or that your initial evaluation needs to be reconsidered. No matter how carefully you've worked, it's always possible that you've overlooked or misinterpreted something. It's also conceivable that you've simply changed your mind, or that an increasing understanding of the subject has altered your earlier conclusions. You shouldn't of course feel restrained by your preliminary decisions.

You can write your paper by following the same steps used for an expository paper:

1. Formulating your ideas
2. Producing a rough draft
3. Producing a final draft

Much of the work of the first step has already been accomplished through the gathering and evaluating of the material. What you need to do now is to organize this material for the paper itself. In doing this, don't feel obligated to use *everything* you've learned in your research. Select only the material that seems appropriate to the central idea and the scope of your paper and then arrange it into a sequence of points that can serve as a preliminary outline.

The writing of your rough draft and the revision of it into a satisfactory final draft can be carried out just as for an expository paper. Your goal, as always, is to achieve effective organization, a clear and concise style, and relative freedom from mechanical errors.

Beyond this you will want to make your paper a successful piece of persuasion. As an overall guide to your purpose in writing a *factual presentation*, it may help to view your task in light of the sort of practical assignment many professional persons are called upon to carry out.

Assume that you're employed as an assistant to a person in a position of some authority—a business executive, a state legislator, a university chancellor, the director of a consumer agency, or the president of a union. An important issue arises, but your employer is too busy to investigate it thoroughly. You're given the job of learning what you can about the matter and submitting a written report that will recommend a position to be taken and provide convincing support for that position. This, in essence, is what a factual presentation assignment asks you to do.

The Personal Opinion Paper

This assignment differs from a factual presentation in that you're not limited to the role of impartial investigator. Instead you're encouraged to explore *your own attitudes and opinions*. The subjects best suited for this type of persuasive writing are usually closely involved with personal experiences, emotional reactions, and broad areas of faith and belief.

Your purpose is not so much to *convince* the reader through a logical and factual presentation as it is to *influence* him by your intelligence, your judgment, your perceptions, the depth of your experience, and the breadth of your understanding.

Possible topics can be listed within certain general areas of human concern:

Religion

Why I am (am not) a Christian, Jew, Moslem, agnostic, atheist, etc.

Politics

Why I am a Democrat, Republican, Socialist, etc.
Why I support (a certain candidate)
Why I favor (oppose) public financing of candidates, the electoral college, a national primary, direct election of judges, more spending for defense (or social programs, education, etc.)

Moral and Social Issues

Abortion
Affirmative action in hiring
The Equal Rights Amendment
Gun control
Strikes by public employees
Pollution
Environmental policies
Open admission to state universities

Personal Preferences

Big colleges versus small
My favorite book, movie, television show, hobby, etc.
What I would change on campus
What was wrong with my high school education
The perfect date
What parents do not understand about their children

Some of these (abortion, direct election of judges, big colleges versus small) could also be treated either as pure exposition or as a factual type of persuasion. The kind of paper you write will depend, in these instances, on the instructor's directions. Most of these topics, however ("What I would change on campus," "Why I am a Christian") are specifically designed for a personal opinion paper.

The sequence for writing this kind of paper is normally:

1. Clarifying your opinion
2. Supporting your opinion
3. Presenting both opinion and support in a convincing manner

Your progress therefore will not usually be from facts to conclusion, as it was before. Rather you will move from a clarification of your opinion to the organization of support for it.

Clarifying Your Opinion
There will be times of course when you will be asked—or will choose—to write on a subject about which you do not have a clear opinion. This means that a certain amount of research (as with the factual presentation paper), or of sorting through your recollections and experiences (for a topic like "what was wrong with my high school education") would have to be done in order to develop your ideas.

However, all of us have strong opinions that we've never explored very fully. Occasionally this puts us in the embarrassing situation of vigorously defending a position only to discover, when pressed, that we're not really sure exactly what that position is.

For this reason, you should begin by phrasing as precisely as you can the subject and main point of your paper. Write them out to make sure you have a clear, concrete grasp of what you intend to say.

Try to limit your subject in accordance with the intended length of the paper. "Pollution," for instance, is obviously a huge subject, and "why I am against pollution" seems to be a poor choice as the main point of a two-page paper. If your initial conception turns out to be this generalized, try to narrow it down by stages. You might progress, for instance, from "pollution," to "air pollution," to "automobile exhausts."

On the basis of this more limited subject, you can then clarify your main point. Since this will reflect your personal opinion, there are of course many possibilities. You could, for instance, take a stand for or against any of the following:

Mass transit
Gas rationing
Higher gas taxes
Controls on the import of oil
Offshore drilling
Controls on the size and horsepower of cars
The development of new fuels
The development of new engines

You could further limit your main point by dealing with various aspects of these issues:

The role of government
The individual's responsibility
The need for social action
The influence of the automobile and petroleum industries

Your purpose through all this should be to develop a clear statement of the opinion you wish to present as the focus of your paper. The more specifically you can phrase it, the clearer it will become in your own mind.

Supporting Your Opinion
The basic difference between this kind of paper and a *factual presentation* is simply that in a *personal opinion* paper your support should be composed of a blend of *both* facts and opinions. The reader is interested in your attitudes, feelings, and convictions and wants you to express them. This doesn't absolve you, however, from your responsibility for factual accuracy and for an honest treatment of your material.

The nature of your subject will largely determine the proportions of this blend of fact and opinion. In areas of personal preference—religion, politics, literary or popular taste—the factual support will obviously be less prominent. At the same time, the reader is looking for something more than a mere statement of preference. *Why*, he wants to know, were you so impressed with a given book? He wants you to expand upon your reactions, to share your pleasures, and to discuss your judgments. Your paper is not merely a device for *stating* your opinions but also, and more importantly, a means of *exploring* these opinions with the reader.

If you were writing on *Crime and Punishment* as your favorite novel, for example, you might organize your support for this preference by analyzing your reactions to certain of the book's qualities. What did you respond to most favorably about the work? What set it above other good novels that you've read? Was it the characterization? The theme? The effectiveness of the scenes? The philosophical implications? The "realness" of the people and events? The universality of the story? The insights of the author?

In other words, you simply should tell your reader more about the way you feel by developing your main idea—that *Crime and Punishment* is your favorite book—into a detailed and extended statement.

Even with topics that depend heavily on factual background—such as "mass transit and air pollution"—your conclusions will largely reflect your own priorities. Do you believe that the personal convenience of the automobile is more (or less) important than the potential benefit, in terms of cleaner air, of mass transit? Should there be some level of acceptable pollution from automobiles before any attempt is made to limit their use? What level should this be, and what forms of restriction should be employed? If mass transit is socially advantageous, how should it be financed? By the users, by local taxation, or by federal funding?

Any discussion of such questions eventually arrives at a point where facts and logic can no longer guide us to an answer, where personal convictions become all-important. These convictions ought to be solidly grounded, but are nonetheless personal and subjective and of course debatable.

To organize support for your opinions, you could start with a clear statement of your main point. Let's assume you wish to take the following position:

Federal support is needed for mass transit.

You could then jot down some of the *factual* material that you think will strengthen your stand:

1. Rising levels of air pollution
2. Increased use of private automobiles
3. Increased congestion in cities
4. Automobiles as inefficient—one or two persons per car
5. Cost per passenger-mile—train and bus versus automobile
6. Energy savings of mass transit
7. Precedent of federal support for other means of transportation—highway funds, airline and ship subsidies, etc.

You may not want to use all of these, especially in a brief paper. Some could be combined, and you can probably think of additional points as you go along. But the list can help you organize your thoughts and can also indicate the extent of your knowledge of the subject. If the evidence that you can cite seems very thin, you may not have enough background to treat the subject effectively. (A topic like "my favorite date" obviously doesn't need much factual support.)

You can then work up a rough list of the kind of value judgments—convictions, opinions, beliefs—upon which your overall conclusion is based:

1. The health of the general public is more important than the convenience of a few.
2. Drivers have no right to pollute the air and harm others.
3. Cities will not only be more healthful but more prosperous if automobile congestion is alleviated.
4. Federal support is justified when social need is great.

Again, you may or may not use all of these, may add others, or may change the phrasing or emphasis as you proceed. At this stage you needn't be concerned about final decisions. You simply want to be sure you know enough about the subject to be able to present reasonable and coherent support for your views.

Presenting Opinion and Support in a Convincing Manner

Since you've given considerable thought to your main idea and to the way you intend to support it, you should be well prepared to undertake the writing of your paper in the usual manner:

1. Formulating your ideas
2. Producing a rough draft
3. Producing a final draft

All you probably need to do for the first step is to organize the supporting points you've listed into an appropriate sequence. Through the next two steps you should pay attention to the same aspects of your writing—organization, style, mechanics—that you would in a piece of pure exposition. Beyond this you should of course try to make the paper effective as a piece of persuasion deserving the attention of an intelligent and knowledgeable reader.

In the preceding section we noted that a *factual presentation* paper requires you to act as an impartial investigator, gathering information and then drawing a logical conclusion from it. A *personal opinion* paper, on the other hand, invites you to assume a role comparable to that of a writer of newspaper editorials, or of columns devoted to political and general commentary. Both the editorial writer and the columnist are expected to express their own views. That is why they are read: People want to see what they have to say. These writers are not necessarily expected to prove their points. Their function is to explore and comment upon issues of both public and personal concern. As readers, we grant them a great deal of freedom in choosing their subjects and espousing their views. At the same time, we expect them to show knowledge of their subjects, respect for the facts, and an ability to express their opinions in a clear and effective manner. This is what your readers expect from you in a *personal opinion* paper.

Considering Your Audience

The need to treat your subject in a manner appropriate to your audience is particularly important in persuasive writing. To make an effective presentation, you must provide your readers with a clear explanation of material that may be unfamiliar to them. At the same time, you shouldn't waste time providing information they already possess.

For example, the amount of background material required for the topic "what I'd change on campus" will be minimal if you are writing for your college classmates, and more extensive if your audience is the senior class at your former high school, most of whom have never seen your campus.

As with your expository papers, if the audience is not specifically defined, you should assume it's composed of persons of intelligence and education with a good general knowledge but little background in specialized fields.

Chapter 9

Reading Imaginative Literature: Stories, Novels, Plays, Poems

The fiction writer, the dramatist, and the poet all deal with fundamental and elusive aspects of human behavior and, ultimately, human existence. The ideal way to respond to literature is the way you do to life itself. When you choose a college, meet your future roommate, go on a blind date, attend a wedding or a funeral, witness an automobile accident, or listen to a Bach concerto, a Dylan song, or a political speech, you react not only to the "facts" of the situation. You respond with your whole being, sensitive to an incredible variety of stimuli from within and without. Literature asks you to do the same.

And just as we can't rely on an "author" in life to tell us what everything "means," neither can we in literature. A successful reader is prepared to figure out things for himself, to explore the moral dilemmas of a work—is Madame Bovary to be praised or blamed for her unconventional behavior?—and finds pleasure in doing so.

Using What You Already Know

Much that you've learned in previous chapters will help you in reading imaginative literature. Here, too, your purpose should determine your approach, for you should not read everything in the same manner, at the same speed, or with the same effort.

You should feel free, for instance, to use on imaginative literature all you have learned about grasping essentials while reading rapidly. Not every story, novel, play, or poem demands exhaustive study, and a skillful rapid reading can result in considerable enjoyment and understanding. Again, though, you should also be able to master thoroughly a piece of imaginative writing when you need or want such mastery.

FICTION: THE SHORT STORY

Since this form is of limited length, a short-story writer works to eliminate all digressions and nonessentials. Typically a short story is severely unified about a single narrative and a single theme. To make the most of what he has, the short-story writer leans heavily on suggestion, implication, and symbolism. He must search not only for the best way to say something, but for the *best, shortest* way. In a short story every word ought to count. You therefore normally should not skip or skim anything but rather try to discover the function of everything in the story.

Practice in Reading Fiction

The following story, by a well-known contemporary American writer, was not chosen as a perfect example of the form, nor to exemplify *all* the things we've been discussing. Each work of literature is unique, presenting its own potential and its own difficulties.

You may find it helpful, though, to bear in mind while reading this story the three basic questions that can help you understand any work of literature:

1. What is happening?
2. Why is it happening?
3. What is its broader significance?

IDIOTS FIRST
Bernard Malamud

> Women and children first.
> OLD SAYING

The thick ticking of the tin clock stopped. Mendel, dozing in the dark, awoke in fright. The pain returned as he listened. He drew on his cold embittered clothing, and wasted minutes sitting at the edge of the bed.

"Isaac," he ultimately sighed.

In the kitchen, Isaac, his astonished mouth open, held six peanuts in his palm. He placed each on the table. "One . . . two . . . nine."

He gathered each peanut and appeared in the doorway. Mendel, in loose hat and long overcoat, still sat on the bed. Isaac watched with small eyes and ears, thick hair graying the sides of his head.

"Schlaf," he nasally said.

'No," muttered Mendel. As if stifling he rose. "Come, Isaac."

He wound his old watch though the sight of the stopped clock nauseated him.

Isaac wanted to hold it to his ear.

"No, it's late." Mendel put the watch carefully away. In the drawer he found the little paper bag of crumpled ones and fives and slipped it into his overcoat pocket. He helped Isaac on with his coat.

Isaac looked at one dark window, then at the other. Mendel stared at both black windows.

They went slowly down the darkly lit stairs, Mendel first, Isaac watching the moving shadows on the wall. To one long shadow he offered a peanut.

"Hungrig."

In the vestibule the old man gazed through the thin glass. The November night was cold and bleak. Opening the door he cautiously thrust his head out. Though he saw nothing he quickly shut the door.

"Ginzburg, that he came to see me yesterday," he whispered in Isaac's ear.

Isaac sucked air.

"You know who I mean?"

Isaac combed his chin with his fingers.

"That's the one, with the black whiskers. Don't talk to him or go with him if he asks you."

Isaac moaned.

"Young people he don't bother so much," Mendel said in afterthought.

It was suppertime and the street was empty but the store windows dimly lit their way to the corner. They crossed the deserted street and went on. Isaac, with a happy cry, pointed to the three golden balls. Mendel smiled but was exhausted when they got to the pawnshop.

The pawnbroker, a red-bearded man with black horn-rimmed glasses, was eating a whitefish at the rear of the store. He craned his head, saw them, and settled back to sip his tea.

In five minutes he came forward, patting his shapeless lips with a large white handkerchief.

Mendel, breathing heavily, handed him the worn gold watch. The pawnbroker, raising his glasses, screwed in his eyepiece. He turned the watch over once. "Eight dollars."

The dying man wet his cracked lips. "I must have thirty-five."

"So go to Rothschild."

"Cost me myself sixty."

"In 1905." The pawnbroker handed back the watch. It had stopped ticking. Mendel wound it slowly. It ticked hollowly.

"Isaac must go to my uncle that he lives in California."

"It's a free country," said the pawnbroker.

Isaac, watching a banjo, snickered.

"What the matter with him?" the pawnbroker asked.

"So let be eight dollars," muttered Mendel, "but where will I get the rest till tonight?"

"How much for my hat and coat?" he asked.

"No sale." The pawnbroker went behind the cage and wrote out a ticket. He locked the watch in a small drawer but Mendel still heard it ticking.

In the street he slipped the eight dollars into the paper bag, then searched in his pockets for a scrap of writing. Finding it, he strained to read the address by the light of the street lamp.

As they trudged to the subway, Mendel pointed to the sprinkled sky.

"Isaac, look how many stars are tonight."

"Eggs," said Isaac.

"First we will go to Mr. Fishbein, after we will eat."

They got off the train in upper Manhattan and had to walk several blocks before they located Fishbein's house.

"A regular palace," Mendel murmured, looking forward to a moment's warmth.

Isaac stared uneasily at the heavy door of the house.

Mendel rang. The servant, a man with long sideburns, came to the door and said Mr. and Mrs. Fishbein were dining and could see no one.

"He should eat in peace but we will wait till he finishes."

"Come back tomorrow morning. Tomorrow morning Mr. Fishbein will talk to you. He don't do business or charity at this time of the night."

"Charity I am not interested—"

"Come back tomorrow."

"Tell him it's life or death—"

"Whose life or death?"

"So if not his, then mine."

"Don't be such a big smart aleck."

"Look me in my face," said Mendel, "and tell me if I got time till tomorrow morning?"

The servant stared at him, then at Isaac, and reluctantly let them in.

The foyer was a vast high-ceilinged room with many oil paintings on the walls, voluminous silken draperies, a thick flowered rug at foot, and a marble staircase.

Mr. Fishbein, a paunchy bald-headed man with hairy nostrils and small patent leather feet, ran lightly down the stairs, a large napkin tucked under a tuxedo coat button. He stopped on the fifth step from the bottom and examined his visitors.

"Who comes on Friday night to a man that he has guests, to spoil him his supper?"

"Excuse me that I bother you, Mr. Fishbein," Mendel said. "If I didn't come now I couldn't come tomorrow."

"Without more preliminaries, please state your business. I'm a hungry man."

"Hungrig," wailed Isaac.

Fishbein adjusted his pince-nez. "What's the matter with him?"

"This is my son Isaac. He is like this all his life." Isaac mewled.

"I am sending him to California."

"Mr. Fishbein don't contribute to personal pleasure trips."

"I am a sick man and he must go tonight on the train to my Uncle Leo."

"I never give to unorganized charity," Fishbein said, "but if you are hungry I will invite you downstairs in my kitchen. We having tonight chicken with stuffed derma."

"All I ask is thirty-five dollars for the train ticket to my uncle in California. I have already the rest."

"Who is your uncle? How old a man?"

"Eighty-one years, a long life to him."

Fishbein burst into laughter. "Eighty-one years and you are sending him this halfwit."

Mendel, flailing both arms, cried, "Please, without names."

Fishbein politely conceded.

"Where is open the door there we go in the house," the sick man said. "If you will kindly give me thirty-five dollars, God will bless you. What is thirty-five dollars to Mr. Fishbein? Nothing. To me, for my boy, is everything."

Fishbein drew himself up to his tallest height.

"Private contributions I don't make—only to insitutions. This is my fixed policy."

Mendel sank to his creaking knees on the rug.

"Please, Mr. Fishbein, if not thirty-five, give maybe twenty."

"Levinson!" Fishbein angrily called.

The servant with the long sideburns appeared at the top of the stairs.

"Show this party where is the door—unless he wishes to partake food before leaving the premises."

"For what I got chicken won't cure it," Mendel said.

"This way if you please," said Levinson, descending.

Isaac assisted his father up.

"Take him to an institution," Fishbein advised over the marble balustrade. He ran quickly up the stairs and they were at once outside, buffeted by winds.

The walk to the subway was tedious. The wind blew mournfully. Mendel, breathless, glanced furtively at shadows. Isaac, clutching his peanuts in his frozen fist, clung to his father's side. They entered a small park to rest for a minute on a stone bench under a leafless two-branched tree. The thick right branch was raised, the thin left one hung down. A very pale moon rose slowly. So did a stranger as they approached the bench.

"Gut yuntif," he said hoarsely.

Mendel, drained of blood, waved his wasted arms. Isaac yowled sickly. Then a bell chimed and it was only ten. Mendel let out a piercing anguished cry as the bearded stranger disappeared into the bushes. A policeman came running, and though he beat the bushes with his nightstick, could turn up nothing. Mendel and Isaac hurried out of the little park. When Mendel glanced back the dead tree had its thin arm raised, the thick one down. He moaned.

They boarded a trolley, stopping at the home of a former friend, but he had died years ago. On the same block they went into a cafeteria and ordered two fried eggs for Isaac. The tables were crowded except where a heavy-set man sat eating soup with kasha. After one look at him they left in haste, although Isaac wept.

Mendel had another address on a slip of paper but the house was too far away, in Queens, so they stood in a doorway shivering.

What can I do, he frantically thought, in one short hour?

He remembered the furniture in the house. It was junk but might bring a few dollars. "Come, Isaac." They went once more to the pawnbroker's to talk to him, but the shop was dark and an iron gate—rings and gold watches glinting through it—was drawn tight across his place of business.

They huddled behind a telephone pole, both freezing. Isaac whimpered.

"See the big moon, Isaac. The whole sky is white."

He pointed but Isaac wouldn't look.

Mendel dreamed for a minute of the sky lit up, long sheets of light in all directions. Under the sky, in California, sat Uncle Leo drinking tea with lemon. Mendel felt warm but woke up cold.

Across the street stood an ancient brick synagogue.

He pounded on the huge door but no one appeared. He waited till he had breath and desperately knocked again. At last there were footsteps within, and the synagogue door creaked open on its massive brass hinges.

A darkly dressed sexton, holding a dripping candle, glared at them.

"Who knocks this time of night with so much noise on the synagogue door?"

Mendel told the sexton his troubles. "Please, I would like to speak to the rabbi."

"The rabbi is an old man. He sleeps now. His wife won't let you see him. Go home and come back tomorrow."

"To tomorrow I said goodbye already. I am a dying man."

Though the sexton seemed doubtful he pointed to an old wooden house next door. "In there he lives." He disappeared into the synagogue with his lit candle casting shadows around him.

Mendel, with Isaac clutching his sleeve, went up the wooden steps and rang the bell. After five minutes a big-faced, gray-haired bulky woman came out on the porch with a torn robe thrown over her nightdress. She emphatically said the rabbi was sleeping and could not be waked.

But as she was insisting, the rabbi himself tottered to the door. He listened a minute and said, "Who wants to see me let them come in."

They entered a cluttered room. The rabbi was an old skinny man with bent shoulders and a wisp of white beard. He wore a flannel nightgown and black skullcap; his feet were bare.

"Vey is mir," his wife muttered. "Put on shoes or tomorrow comes sure pneumonia." She was a woman with a big belly, years younger than her husband. Staring at Isaac, she turned away.

Mendel apologetically related his errand. "All I need more is thirty-five dollars."

"Thirty-five?" said the rabbi's wife. "Why not thirty-five thousand? Who has so much money? My husband is a poor rabbi. The doctors take away every penny."

"Dear friend," said the rabbi, "if I had I would give you."

"I got already seventy," Mendel said, heavy-hearted, "All I need more is thirty-five."

"God will give you," said the rabbi.

"In the grave," said Mendel. "I need tonight. Come, Isaac."

"Wait," called the rabbi.

He hurried inside, came out with a fur-lined caftan, and handed it to Mendel.

"Yascha," shrieked his wife, "not your new coat!"

"I got my old one. Who needs two coats for one body?"

"Yascha, I am screaming—"

"Who can go among poor people, tell me, in a new coat?"

"Yascha," she cried, "what can this man do with your coat? He needs tonight the money. The pawnbrokers are asleep."

"So let him wake them up."

"No." She grabbed the coat from Mendel.

He held on to a sleeve, wrestling her for the coat. Her I know, Mendel thought. "Shylock," he muttered. Her eyes glittered.

The rabbi groaned and tottered dizzily. His wife cried out as Mendel yanked the coat from her hands.

"Run," cried the rabbi.

"Run, Isaac."

They ran out of the house and down the steps.

"Stop, you thief," called the rabbi's wife.

The rabbi pressed both hands to his temples and fell to the floor.

"Help!" his wife wept. "Heart attack! Help!"

But Mendel and Isaac ran through the streets with the rabbi's new fur-lined caftan. After them noiselessly ran Ginzburg.

It was very late when Mendel bought the train ticket in the only booth open.

There was no time to stop for a sandwich so Isaac ate his peanuts and they hurried to the train in the vast deserted station.

"So in the morning," Mendel gasped as they ran, "there comes a man that he sells sandwiches and coffee. Eat but get change. When reaches California the train will be waiting for you on the station Uncle Leo. If you don't recognize him he will recognize you. Tell him I send best regards."

But when they arrived at the gate to the platform it was shut, the light out.

Mendel, groaning, beat on the gate with his fists.

"Too late," said the uniformed ticket collector, a bulky, bearded man with hairy nostrils and a fishy smell.

He pointed to the station clock. "Already past twelve."

"But I see standing there still the train," Mendel said, hopping in his grief.

"It just left—in one more minute."

"A minute is enough. Just open the gate."

"Too late I told you."

Mendel socked his bony chest with both hands. "With my whole heart I beg you this little favor."

"Favors you had enough already. For you the train is gone. You shoulda been dead already at midnight. I told you that yesterday. This is the best I can do."

"Ginzburg!" Mendel shrank from him.

"Who else?" The voice was metallic, eyes glittered, the expression amused.

"For myself," the old man begged, "I don't ask a thing. But what will happen to my boy?"

Ginzburg shrugged slightly. "What will happen happens. This isn't my responsibility. I got enough to think about without worrying about somebody on one cylinder."

"What then is your responsibility?"

"To create conditions. To make happen what happens. I ain't in the anthropomorphic business."

"Whatever business you in, where is your pity?"

"This ain't my commodity. The law is the law."

"Which law is this?"

"The cosmic universal law, goddamit, the one I got to follow myself."

"What kind of a law is it?" cried Mendel. "For God's sake, don't you understand what I went through in my life with this poor boy? Look at him. For thirty-nine years, since the day he was born, I wait for him to grow up, but he don't. Do you understand what this means in a father's heart? Why don't you let him go to his uncle?" His voice had risen and he was shouting.

Isaac mewled loudly.

"Better calm down or you'll hurt somebody's feelings," Ginzburg said with a wink toward Isaac.

"All my life," Mendel cried, his body trembling, "what did I have? I was poor. I suffered from my health. When I worked I worked too hard. When I didn't work was worse. My wife died a young woman. But I didn't ask from anybody nothing. Now I ask a small favor. Be so kind, Mr. Ginzburg."

The ticket collector was picking his teeth with a match stick.

"You ain't the only one, my friend, some got it worse than you. That's how it goes in this country."

"You dog you." Mendel lunged at Ginzburg's throat and began to choke. "You bastard, don't you understand what it means human?"

They struggled nose to nose, Ginzburg, though his astonished eyes bulged, began to laugh. "You pipsqueak nothing. I'll freeze you to pieces."

His eyes lit in rage and Mendel felt an unbearable cold like an icy dagger invading his body, all of his parts shriveling.

Now I die without helping Isaac.

A crowd gathered. Isaac yelped in fright.

Clinging to Ginzburg in his last agony, Mendel saw reflected in the ticket collector's eyes the depth of his terror. But he saw that Ginzburg, staring at himself in Mendel's eyes, saw mirrored in them the extent of his own awful wrath. He beheld a shimmering, starry, blinding light that produced darkness.

Ginzburg looked astounded. "Who me?"

His grip on the squirming old man slowly loosened, and Mendel, his heart barely beating, slumped to the ground.

"Go," Ginzburg muttered, "take him to the train."

"Let pass," he commanded a guard.

The crowd parted. Isaac helped his father up and they tottered down the steps to the platform where the train waited, lit and ready to go.

Mendel found Isaac a coach seat and hastily embraced him. "Help Uncle Leo, Isaakil. Also remember your father and mother."

"Be nice to him," he said to the conductor. "Show him where everything is."

He waited on the platform until the train began slowly to move. Isaac sat at the edge of his seat, his face strained in the direction of his journey. When the train was gone, Mendel ascended the stairs to see what had become of Ginzburg.

An Approach to Bernard Malamud's "Idiots First"

Although relatively simple on the surface, "Idiots First" rewards the alert reader by gradually revealing its deeper concerns. But even a brief look—something on the order of a preliminary survey—will indicate certain distinctive qualities of the work. We can then proceed to develop gradually a fuller response to the three basic questions that ought to be asked about a work of literature: (1) *What is happening?* (2) *Why is it happening?* (3) *What is its broader significance?*

What Is Happening?
We shouldn't have too much trouble developing a brief summary of the narrative:

> Mendel, an old man convinced of the imminence of his death, spends a frantic evening collecting money to send his retarded son, Isaac, to the safekeeping of an uncle in California.

We'll expand and correct this summary as we go along, our goal being a full understanding of everything that happens in the work. One way of achieving this is to consider Malamud's story in terms of traditional narrative structure. In general, a controlled narrative—as opposed to one that is aimless, pointless, or disorganized—proceeds through four stages:

1. Exposition
2. Increasing tension
3. Climax
4. Resolution

The *exposition* informs the reader about the setting, characters, time, and locale of the narrative situation. It's the background needed to understand the story.

We can quickly fill in the important background information provided by Malamud. The setting is obviously New York City, as indicated by references to "upper Manhattan" and "Queens." The names and speech patterns of the characters, along with the presence of the rabbi, make clear that they're all Jewish.

We also learn some particulars about the father and son. "For thirty-nine years, since the day he was born, I wait for him to grow up, but he don't," Mendel says of Isaac. Mendel further informs us that he is a widower whose wife "died a young woman." From this information, presented quite directly, certain things about their relationship are implied. For instance, it appears that Mendel has had full responsibility for Isaac throughout most of his son's life. And since there's no mention of other children, Isaac has probably been the *sole* focus of Mendel's life for many years. These implications help explain Mendel's ferocious dedication to his son's welfare.

The title can often provide helpful clues to the author's concerns, especially after you've gained some preliminary knowledge of the story. In this case, Malamud offers as a headnote the old saying, "Women and children first," to suggest how we should read the title. Just as women and children were traditionally rescued from a sinking ship, even at the cost of the lives of the men, so we see Mendel willing to accept his own death if only he can save his retarded son.

Both from several specific allusions and from Mendel's difficulty in raising the money he needs, it's clear that he's a poor man who's worked hard all his life for what little he has.

All this background information, both stated and implied, is readily accessible to an active reader. We mention it simply to illustrate the sort of preliminary understanding that will prepare you for a fuller reading of the work.

Before we go on, though, we should take a closer look at one of the expository elements readers sometimes find troublesome. As we've mentioned, the characters in "Idiots First" speak a kind of New York City dialect heavily influenced by Yiddish phrasing. "For what I got chicken won't cure it," Mendel says, referring to his imminent death in declining Fishbein's offers of a free meal. If you're not familiar with this pattern of speech, you may find some of Malamud's dialogue hard to understand at first. Trying to "hear" it should help, and most readers can pick up the rhythms and the flavor of an unfamiliar *patois* with a little effort.

Malamud is typical of many writers in his concern for the accurate rendering of the locale, the way of life, and the unique speech of his characters. For most of us this realistic recreation is one of the attractions of fiction, introducing us to people we do not know and ways of life distant from our own. Beyond that, an author's skill in reproducing the real speech of his characters contributes greatly to the convincing sense of "life" that fiction offers.

A period of *increasing tension* is produced by the conflict between opposing forces that normally occurs in a controlled narrative. This conflict may be external—between people, between groups of people, or between people and natural or man-made forces. It may be internal—between opposing attitudes, philosophies, or wills within the mind of a character. But a conflict is almost always present, allowing the narrative to move through a period of heightening tension toward an inevitable confrontation.

The conflict of "Idiots First" quite clearly seems to be between Mendel's overwhelming determination to save his son by sending him to California and the fact that, on the verge of death, he lacks the money to do so.

In any narrative it's helpful to define the basic conflict, since it generally serves as the focus of the work. A simple illustration can help you do this. Start by identifying the first two elements—the protagonist, or main character, and the goal he wishes to achieve (Figure 9-1). This doesn't produce a conflict, however. If Mendel were rich and/or healthy, he'd have no problem sending Isaac to California, and we'd have no story, or at least a very different one. The essential third element needed to produce conflict is something—a person, a situation, or a set of circumstances—that prevents the protagonist from *easily* achieving his goal. This is generally referred to as the barrier or the obstacle, as shown in Figure 9-2.

In "Idiots First," as we've noted, Mendel's poverty and the nearness of his death combine to serve as the barrier. The fact that he can't overcome these obstacles without considerable effort gives the story its constantly increasing tension. With time growing short and his frustrations rising, Mendel desperately tries one way after another to achieve his goal. He pawns his watch, hoping to raise the thirty-five dollars he needs, but gets only eight. He tries to pawn his hat and coat, but they're obviously worthless. He pleads for money from Mr. Fishbein, an apparent stranger. Even getting to speak to Fishbein presents a challenge. Mendel must first get past the servant and does so only by convincing the man of the seriousness of his plight. But Fishbein has a "fixed policy" against private contributions and turns Mendel down.

He goes to the home of a former friend but learns he has been dead for years. Although he has "another address on a slip of paper," the man lives too far away. "What can I do, he frantically thought, in one short hour?"

As a last resort he goes to a synagogue and again has to struggle just to get past the sexton. He learns to his dismay that the rabbi has no money to give. But Mendel's grief touches the rabbi, who offers him his new coat. The solution finally seems within grasp when another obstacle appears in the person of the rabbi's outraged wife. She berates her husband for his foolishness, protests that the pawnshops are all closed anyhow, and tries to seize the coat. In a terrifying scene Mendel wrests it from her and flees, as the rabbi, overwrought from the excitement, collapses to the floor.

From beginning to end, Mendel's quest is marked by frustration and failure. At the same time, his passionate determination to succeed blots out his normal human feelings. He becomes so obsessed that he is reduced to wrestling with a woman. Having gained his prize, he doesn't even pause to offer help to the stricken rabbi, the one person who has shown him any generosity.

The structure illustrated by these incidents is typical of a great many stories, in that the initial conflict becomes more complicated as the protagonist struggles to achieve his goal. It needn't be, as it is for Mendel, a question of life or death. But it's generally a matter of some importance to the character and a reflection of the central concerns of the author.

There's another element that contributes, more subtly, to the increasing tension of Mendel's search. What can we make, at this point, of Ginzburg? He appears—or seems to appear—on several occasions, although it's not wholly clear at first just how he functions in the story.

The earliest mention of Ginzburg, in fact, seems to be deliberately mysterious:

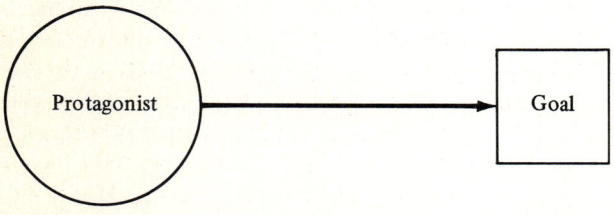

Figure 9-1

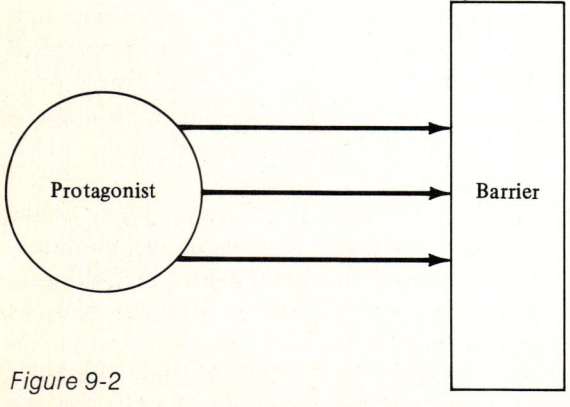 

Figure 9-2

> . . . Opening the door he [Mendel] cautiously thrust his head out. Though he saw nothing he quickly shut the door.
> "Ginzburg, that he came to see me yesterday," he whispered in Isaac's ear.
> Isaac sucked air.
> "You know who I mean?"
> Isaac combed his chin with his fingers.
> "That's the one, with the black whiskers. Don't talk to him or go with him if he asks you."
> Isaac moaned.
> "Young people he don't bother so much," Mendel said in afterthought.

The reactions of both father and son suggest an unmistakable threat. Mendel looks out "cautiously" and shuts the door immediately even though he doesn't see anything. When he tells Isaac who he's looking for, he "whispers" the name in his ear. Isaac shows his uneasiness by sucking in air and moaning.

Ginzburg is not mentioned again by name until near the end of the story, when Mendel and Isaac are running from the synagogue with the rabbi's coat. With no preparation, we're simply told, "After them noiselessly ran Ginzburg."

Then we discover that the uniformed ticket collector, who at first refuses to let Isaac board the train, is Ginzburg. Mendel engages him in a furious exchange, carried on in an odd mixture of street talk and "philosophical" discourse. Ginzburg thus materializes as yet another obstacle that Mendel must overcome, and the scene becomes the ultimate confrontation between Mendel, the protagonist, and Ginzburg, the final and most threatening of the difficulties that have beset him.

What we have come to, then, is the *climax* of the story, in which the tensions that have been increasing are finally, one way or another, resolved in a head-on clash between the opposing forces.

The final stage of the narrative, the *resolution*, can now be identified, for the moment at least, as Mendel's achievement of his goal: the safe placement of Isaac on the train to California.

We have thus developed a broad, although still preliminary outline of *what* happens in the story in terms of its basic narrative development. As we go on to consider *why* these things happen, we should be able to extend this knowledge considerably, revising our initial impressions whenever necessary.

In reading a literary work, you'll of course often deal with all three questions at the same time, since what happens is inevitably bound up with why it happens and with its broader significance. For our purposes, though, we'll separate these three questions in order to illustrate a general procedure which can be used with whatever variations you find helpful.

Why Is It Happening?

In most stories, the best place to look for reasons *why* things happen as they do is in the most important part of the narrative, the climax, where the two major participants in the conflict are usually pitted against one another.

The importance of Ginzburg in the climactic scene of "Idiots First" offers a good example of this. For most readers, the emergence of Ginzburg as a vital force in the story comes as something of a surprise. He's been mentioned only twice up to this point, and before he appears at the railroad station the reader hardly knows anything about him.

This apparent inconsistency—having a seemingly minor character assume such importance in the climax—should alert us to the possibility that we may have missed something along the way.

The possibility always exists of course that the author has been careless, in this case perhaps by failing to develop Ginzburg effectively, or by producing a story marred by structural inconsistencies. But before we assume the author is at fault, we should first try to understand the story as fully as we can.

Are there any clues to the importance of Ginzburg that we have overlooked?

Turning to the story again, we see that two unidentified characters are introduced, both of whom produce a violent reaction in Mendel. These characters appear only fleetingly, and the author doesn't offer an explanation of their significance. It's up to us, then, to seek out suggestions and implications.

The first stranger to appear has a startling effect on both Mendel and Isaac, and even on the natural surroundings. Father and son, having just been rebuffed by Fishbein, stop to rest in a small park. Just before this, Mendel "glanced furtively at shadows," apparently still as fearful as when he earlier looked outside the door of the house.

> . . . They entered a small park to rest for a minute on a stone bench under a leafless two-branched tree. The thick right branch was raised, the thin left one hung down. A very pale moon rose slowly. So did a stranger as they approached the bench.
> "Gut yuntif," he said hoarsely.
> Mendel, drained of blood, waved his wasted arms. Isaac yowled sickly. Then a bell chimed and it was only ten. Mendel let out a piercing anguished cry as the bearded stranger disappeared into the bushes. A policeman came running, and though he beat the bushes with his nightstick, could turn up nothing. Mendel and Isaac hurried out of the little

park. When Mendel glanced back the dead tree had its thin arm raised, the thick one down. He moaned.

Surely the reversal of the tree branches signifies something, as does the stranger's greeting. "Gut yuntif" is a Yiddish salutation roughly translated as "Good holiday." It is used only on holy days, and Mendel, aware of its inappropriateness on a normal day, is obviously shaken.

In the very next paragraph, father and son enter a cafeteria where all the tables are crowded "except where a heavyset man sat eating soup with kasha. After one look at him they left in haste, although Isaac wept."

There seem to be at least three concrete parallels between these two men and Ginzburg. First, Mendel and Isaac react in the same way to all three: with howls, shrieks, or moans. Then there's the emphasis, in the initial mention of Ginzburg, on his beard, and on the fact that the first stranger is also bearded. Finally, all three are presented as mysterious, shadowy figures.

Clearly, then, we ought to consider the possibility that the three characters are related—or perhaps even the same person. Since the author doesn't make this connection for us, we should proceed cautiously. If some relationship exists, it depends wholly on implication. How strong, then, is the implication?

If these three people are *all* Ginzburg, it would at least explain the apparent structural weakness we mentioned earlier, which is the disappearance of Ginzburg between the first mention of him and his sudden emergence as a key figure at the end. What this interpretation gives us is a fairly regular sequence of mentions and appearances throughout the story, culminating in the very last line, when we're told that Mendel "ascended the stairs to see what had become of Ginzburg."

Thus we have, in addition to the parallels suggested by the beard, the mysterious introductions, and the fearful reactions, a further consistency in the structural pattern of their appearance.

One more point can be cited in support of this interpretation. Up to the incident in the park, the story maintains a convincingly realistic tone, without any suggestion of unworldly events. The mysterious transformation of the tree, though, abruptly changes the *kind* of story we are reading. Although the realistic narrative continues, we now see that the author has introduced supernatural elements and that the story cannot therefore be viewed as pure realism.

If the stranger in the park is indeed Ginzburg, we would expect to see this supernatural emphasis borne out in Ginzburg's overall development. We would also expect it to help explain why Ginzburg acts as he does, and why Mendel and Isaac view him with such terror.

There's a fairly strong suggestion that Ginzburg is more than a mere human in the manner in which he pursues Mendel throughout the story. More importantly, the climactic scene at the railway station seems filled with hints of superhuman knowledge and power on his part.

For one thing, the man who only a short time before was chasing Mendel and his son along the street has now suddenly materialized as a uniformed ticket taker. Then we notice that Mendel, who's obviously seen Ginzburg before, and who's in such fear of him that he would hardly forget what he looks like, doesn't even recognize him at first. Apparently Ginzburg can change his appearance when he wishes to, either through disguises or some magical power. Why, though, does he bother to do this? And why does he expend so much time and effort chasing after a poor and dying man? We're given no realistic answers by the author, again suggesting that the answer must be sought on another level.

The interchange between Ginzburg and Mendel seems to reinforce this otherworldly quality. "You shoulda been dead already at midnight," Ginzburg tells Mendel. "I told you that yesterday. This is the best I can do." Later he says that his responsibility is "to create conditions. To make happen what happens," and that his "commodity" is the "cosmic universal law." As they struggle, Ginzburg taunts Mendel: "You pipsqueak nothing. I'll freeze you to pieces." Instantly Mendel feels "an unbearable cold like an icy dagger invading his body."

The final indication of Ginzburg's extraordinary powers occurs in the already-cited last line of the story, when Mendel goes "to see what had become of Ginzburg." It's hard to think of any realistic reason why Mendel, after fleeing from Ginzburg in mortal terror throughout the story, should now calmly seek out his tormentor.

We can test this reading of the story by seeing if we can find some *other* explanation that is equally plausible. Perhaps one exists, and it's always possible that someone of greater intelligence, perception, or sensitivity, can discover it. At the same time, we shouldn't be so cautious that we shy away from any interpretation at all. As in any situation demanding judgment, we simply have to do the best we can to understand the "facts" at hand.

To view Ginzburg as a realistic character and accept the two unidentified men as nothing more than casual strangers would rob the story of both structural and thematic coherence. It would also leave unexplained the change in the tree limbs, Ginzburg's motives in pursuing Mendel, Ginzburg's power to "freeze" Mendel, and the reason why Mendel seeks out Ginzburg at the end.

We can further test the interpretation we have set forth by seeing whether it can help us answer the questions we have been considering: *why* the characters behave as they do, and *why* the events occur as they do.

Again we should be careful to work from the story itself, rather than from our own preconceptions, by determining the central concerns (or themes or motifs) of the author.

Mendel's imminent death probably comes to mind first. From beginning to end it is the overwhelming "fact" that drives Mendel to behave as he does. His son, after all, has been the same for thirty-nine years. Only now, with death staring him in the face, does Mendel resort to the feverish activity that we witness in the story.

A preoccupation with death is stated directly several times in the story, and we're provided with further indication of its crucial importance by more subtle references in the opening paragraphs. We're told in the first sentence that the "clock stopped," and in the second that Mendel, who had been dozing "awoke in fright." "The pain returned" immediately, and Mendel "wasted minutes" sitting on the bed. A few paragraphs later the author says that "the sight of the stopped clock nauseated him."

On first reading, these details may not seem very significant. As with a challenging piece of exposition or persuasion, we often have to gain some knowledge of the work as a whole before we can understand all the details. Given the story's preoccupation with death, Mendel's twice-mentioned dismay at the idea of a clock stopping seems to suggest his overwhelming concern with the fact that his life—his own "clock"—is soon about to stop. And the few minutes spent sitting on the bed are "wasted," because he has not used them to move closer to his goal before his string of precious minutes runs out.

The emphasis on death, if it is central to our understanding of the story, should also help us deal with the main problem that remains—the role of Ginzburg. The first hint of Ginzburg's relation to the idea of death comes in the initial mention of him that we quoted earlier. After Mendel warns his son to stay away from the man and not to "go with him if he asks you," he adds an afterthought that now seems more meaningful than it did before: "Young people he don't bother so much." Obviously old people like Mendel are most likely to be visited by death.

The association of Ginzburg with death also seems to explain his use of "Gut yuntif" as his greeting in the park, and Mendel's shock at hearing it. There's no mention of a holiday in the story. The only thing special about this day is that it has been foreordained, as Mendel clearly assumes, as the day of his death. The "Good holiday" greeting therefore is not only ironic, but also a sign to Mendel that Ginzburg is intimately involved in the only thing—Mendel's impending death—that makes this day special.

We can now look more closely at what we learn about Ginzburg at the railroad station, where he appears as the final obstacle between Mendel and his goal. In realistic terms, Ginzburg controls the physical access to the train, in the form of a locked gate. But the fierce dialogue between the two men reveals an additional symbolic role for Ginzburg, in that he also seems to be intimately involved in the single overriding obstacle Mendel must overcome: his impending death. Ginzburg says "You shoulda been dead already at midnight. . . . This is the best I can do." It's precisely at that moment, when Ginzburg claims authority in determining the time of Mendel's demise, that Mendel recognizes him for the first time.

Thus, on a realistic level, Mendel begs Ginzburg to open the gate. On a more supernatural level, he pleads for the few more moments of life he needs to put Isaac on the train. Ginzburg's connection with Mendel's death is reinforced when, in their struggle, he threatens to "freeze" Mendel—a fairly universal metaphor for death—and Mendel actually feels an "unbearable cold" throughout his body. Mendel himself accepts this as a sign that his life is ending, for he thinks, "Now I die without helping Isaac."

At the climactic moment of the story, then, we receive strong confirmation that Ginzburg is a supernatural being whose role it is to announce, and probably also bring about, Mendel's demise. Something causes Ginzburg to relent, however:

> . . . Ginzburg, staring at himself in Mendel's eyes, saw mirrored in them the extent of his own awful wrath. He beheld a shimmering, starry, blinding light that produced darkness.
> Ginzburg looked astounded. "Who me?"

He loosens his grip on the old man and mutters with a kind of grudging resignation, "Go . . . take him to the train."

What causes this turnabout? It seems apparent that he has been overruled by some higher power. If Ginzburg is to be taken as a sort of "angel of death," this higher power, with ultimate control over matters of life and death, can be seen as "God" in some form or other.

This interpretation also explains Mendel's puzzling behavior in the last sentence in the story, when he goes to seek out Ginzburg instead of trying to escape from him. Mendel realizes that he was granted only enough time to save Isaac. And that is all that he wanted. Now that he has achieved his goal, he is content to surrender himself to Ginzburg because he is not giving in to a human enemy but to the symbolic embodiment of his own preordained death.

It is worthwhile to recall here the comment made in an earlier chapter, to the effect that in all forms of writing the most important parts are usually the beginning and the end, and that these parts are usually reserved for matters of prime importance. In "Idiots First," both the opening sentences, where Mendel wakes up in fright when the clock stops ticking, and the closing sentence, where he goes off to seek Ginzburg, emphasize—although in symbolic terms—the theme of Mendel's death.

We should now, before considering the final question of the story's broader significance, try to state more fully our initial perceptions of the elements of the story. The increasing tension, for instance, depends not only on the realistic sequence of events in which Mendel tries to raise the money he needs, but also on the recurring image of Ginzburg, as death, pursuing Mendel every step of the way. And the climax, we can now say, occurs when Mendel actually wrestles with this representation of his death. Through "God's" intervention, he forestalls Ginzburg long enough to put Isaac on the train. This serves, on the realistic level, as the story's resolution, although we can now add another element to the resolution: Mendel's acceptance of his fate. Having accomplished his goal, he is now ready to return to Ginzburg and accept death without regret.

What Is Its Broader Significance?

As we progress through these three questions, we're obviously moving from relatively factual matters into areas that are considerably more abstract and debatable. Since a good part of the function of literature is simply to make us think, react, and feel, we needn't always demand that a story present some kind of moral. Because we can't neatly sum up the "meaning" of a work doesn't mean that it has failed, or that we've not gained anything from it. If a story moves us, stirs us, allows us to see things in a fresh way, or offers us a glimpse into the lives of people we are made to care about—that can often be enough to satisfy both writer and reader.

At the same time, many writers *are* obviously dealing with certain universal aspects of human existence, and we should make an honest effort to discover what they have to say.

The climactic scene is again a good place to look for clues about a story's broader significance. In the confrontation at the railroad station, our view of Ginzburg as a kind of emissary of "God" is supported by his insistence that all he does is carry out the "cosmic universal law." When Mendel asks, "Where is your pity?" Ginzburg says, "This ain't my commodity." He is, in other words, merely a functionary, a man who follows orders and does a job without concerning himself about such "commodities" as pity. In his final desperate fury, Mendel lunges at Ginzburg and tries to throttle him. "You bastard, don't you understand what it means human?"

Mendel's ultimate accusation, therefore, is that Ginzburg doesn't even know what it means to be human, to be a person, to feel and love and have pity. Thus we see Mendel as a single tormented individual, and an unexceptional one at that, a poor man who has achieved little in his life, pleading in the face of death for some sign of "human" qualities in a world that has treated him only as an insignificant speck in a vast cosmos. Where, he demands of Ginzburg, as he has throughout this exchange, can a man find kindness and love, mercy and charity? Earlier Ginzburg had said, "I ain't in the anthropomorphic business." Here, certainly, is a case where one's understanding of a key word is necessary. Webster's *New World Dictionary* defines anthropomorphism as "the attributing of human shape or characteristics to gods, objects, animals . . . ." In this context, the reference is obviously to the anthropomorphic concept of a God that not only is in the shape of a man but also possesses the characteristics humans have consistently attributed to such a God, who is seen as kindly and paternal and whose "eye is on the sparrow." It is a God who watches with sympathy over all living creatures.

It is this concept that Ginzburg rejects by saying that he's not in the "anthropomorphic business." But moments later he beholds a "shimmering, starry, blinding light" mirrored in Mendel's eyes and takes it as a sign, a command, from the authority that rules over him.

What is signified by this strange light in Mendel's eyes? Perhaps, Malamud seems to be suggesting, it is a confirmation that God's humanity manifests itself even in the most insignificant of human beings. We don't have to accept the author's convictions in this matter, but it does seem clear that Mendel's story, as depressing as it might be considered, is not to be taken merely as a pathetic recounting of an insignificant man's death, but rather as an affirmation that, even in a life filled with sadness and frustration, there is still the assurance, or at least the hope, that the world is watched over by a God capable of pity and kindness. Although neither Mendel's resignation to death nor Isaac's somewhat ambiguous future with the uncle in California makes for a happy ending, it seems clear that Malamud's ultimate purpose in telling us their story is not simply to remind us of the pain and deprivation of their particular lives, and of all our lives, but to suggest that our fate is determined by more than a toss of the dice. To be human, he is saying, is to be touched in ways beyond our understanding by a mysterious but ultimately humane God.

The Literary Qualities of Fiction

We've spent a good deal of time discussing what could be called the "content" of "Idiots First." Before we move on to other literary forms, we should remind ourselves that literature appeals to us—and indeed exists—because it achieves an effect that transcends its content. A good story, like any successful work of art, is more than the sum of its parts. Even if we assume that our analysis of "Idiots First" is acceptable—which may or may not be true—we have to keep in mind that we've dealt with only one aspect of the author's total achievement. A story succeeds because it does more than simply "say" something to us. As readers, we should be able to respond to the qualities of artistic merit that give a literary work its distinctive effectiveness.

The concept of artistic merit is an elusive one and has to be approached gingerly. But it may be helpful to use our familiarity with Malamud's story to suggest some of the ways in which an accomplished writer creates a work designed not only to be understood but also to be experienced.

For our purposes, we can simply take a look at Malamud's use of two of the distinctive elements of literature.

Implication. Through implications, hints, suggestions, images, and symbols, a writer can say a great deal in a few words. It takes a lot longer, as we've seen, to explain Ginzburg's role in the story than it does for Malamud to create that role for us. Implication also encourages the reader to react to certain stimuli without being limited or directed by the writer. When Mendel demands of Ginzburg, "Don't you understand what it means human?" we're being guided toward a consideration of what it *does* mean to be human, on our own terms and in reference to our beliefs and experiences. The author doesn't tell us what our response should be, but rather encourages us to *have* responses.

Implication thus requires the reader to become actively involved in the story. Much of the expository information presented by Malamud, as we've pointed out, is implied rather than stated. In order to find out what we need to know, we have to put together the clues on our own, thereby becoming participants in the creation of the story's effect rather than simply passive recipients. Even points as vital as the supernatural role of Ginzburg have to be actively sought out. And the fact that Mendel is near death and that Isaac is retarded—although both are later stated directly—are first implied by the author. In Mendel's case we have several references to a stopped clock, while our first view of Isaac shows him with his "astonished mouth open," holding six peanuts in his hand. He places them on the table and counts, "One . . . two . . . nine." Mendel's condition is implied quite subtly, Isaac's rather obviously, but in neither instance does the author *tell* us what to think. We're instead encouraged to become active readers and are later treated to the pleasure of having our earlier inferences confirmed.

In simpler forms like the detective story, our surmises are generally confined to clear-cut questions of guilt or innocence. In more complex literary works, we're prompted to grapple with more intricate and ambiguous questions. The principle, though, is the same. Being told something is a lot less stimulating, and a lot less fun, than figuring it out for ourselves.

Malamud's symbolic use of the stopped clocks, the tree limbs, and in a broader sense Ginzburg's role as the "angel of death," are all presented as concrete embodiments of more generalized or abstract concepts. As such, they allow us to proceed from an initial awareness of objects and people to a discovery, largely on our own, of the significance they possess.

Organic unity. Earlier we spoke of fiction as a controlled narrative in which the elements are fused into an organic whole. In Malamud's story, this strict unity can be exemplified by the ordering of the narrative elements. The story moves rapidly, and without digression, from an early presentation of the central conflict through a period of increasing tension to a climax and resolution.

Not every story, naturally, exhibits such a clear line of narrative development. Many contemporary writers minimize, or eliminate entirely, the conventional narrative elements in order to experiment with new and sometimes puzzling forms. Instead of a recognizable sequence of events, these works often depend on a mood, a locale, a point of view, a creation of an individual consciousness, or some other unifying focus. The important point is that even these highly individualistic approaches to fiction are in most cases organized into a coherent pattern of some sort. In a successful story, whether traditional or experimental, the artistic unity of the work is achieved through the presentation, directly or indirectly, of everything that is needed, and the exclusion of everything that is extraneous. We're given only that which is essential to the narrative or thematic focus.

In "Idiots First," for example, we're not told what work Mendel has done all his life. Nor are we offered any description of his apartment, his building, or his neighborhood. We learn nothing about his wife except that she died young. We're given very little in the way of a physical description of the characters.

In many stories these matters are treated at great length. They aren't in this story because Malamud obviously doesn't feel they are necessary to his total effect. An unskilled writer often feels obligated to describe everything that is "there"—apartments, houses, neighborhoods, characters. An accomplished writer, however, concentrates on what is needed for the particular effect he wants.

For this reason, we're given only a few details about Isaac's appearance: his "astonished mouth" and his "small eyes and ears, thick hair graying the sides of his head." We're not told whether he's tall or short, thin or fat. What we are told, though, contributes significantly to the essential knowledge we must have about him—his retardation and the fact that, although he speaks and acts like a child, he is thirty-nine years old.

The same can be said of the setting. There's only one tree in the story, and one clump of bushes. Neither is introduced merely to set the scene. Both are important to our understanding of the work, for in a well-crafted story all the characters play a role, and so do all the objects. Everything contributes. Organic unity is achieved when the central concerns of the author—the theme, the story, the motifs—determine what belongs and what doesn't. Nothing is included unless it has a function.

This stringent selectivity produces the *compression* that is a distinctive element of short fiction. A story's pace tends to be rapid, because everything has been eliminated that might impede its forward progress.

In "Idiots First," for example, Malamud leaves out a scene that in practical terms is quite important. After Mendel flees from the synagogue with the rabbi's coat, noiselessly pursued by Ginzburg, he obviously has to convert the garment into cash. Earlier the rabbi's wife mentioned that the pawnbrokers are all closed. "So let him wake them up," the rabbi responds. And that, we have to assume, is what happens. Mendel goes to a pawnbroker, rouses him out of bed, and obtains the money he needs.

This action is crucial to the story; it's here that Mendel finally acquires the money needed for the train ticket. Yet the scene doesn't exist. One paragraph ends with Ginzburg pursuing him, and the next begins with, "It was very late when Mendel bought the ticket...."

It should be obvious why Malamud has declined to write this scene for us. We can "write" it ourselves. What happens during this time has been so clearly implied that the author feels justified in leaving it out and moving directly to the climax. The story's demand for unity and compression requires only that the author tell us everything that is necessary, not everything that happens.

Reading Short Stories: Some Final Suggestions

It's important to remember that, although all stories share certain characteristics, each possesses its own unique qualities. Rather than trying to fit a story into a preconceived mold, you should instead always work toward a recognition of its individual concerns, its particular structure, and its singular achievement.

To help you do this, you may want to keep in mind some of the general principles we've set forth:

1. As with exposition and persuasion, you should first try to gain at least a preliminary knowledge of the overall structure and basic concerns of a story before worrying about details.
2. Use your time, whenever possible, for several alert readings, building each time on the knowledge gained from previous readings and actively seeking to fill in the gaps in your understanding. Not all stories require this sort of extended study. Spend as much time as you need for the level of understanding you want.
3. Without letting the format inhibit you, try to proceed toward an increasingly detailed understanding of what happens, why it happens, and what its broader significance is.
4. Use your knowledge of the conventional narrative pattern to determine, at least in general terms, the central conflict, the pattern of developing tension, and the climax and resolution of the story. Remember that the climax, especially, can reveal a great deal about the work as a whole, since it frequently involves the major characters, the basic conflict, and the central theme of the story.
5. Be receptive to suggestion and implication. Rely as much as possible on the text itself to provide you with the clues you need.

6. Since most well-written stories are tightly compressed and unified, try to understand the role of everything that appears in the story.
7. Remember, finally, that a story is not an essay, not a political tract, and not a philosophical discourse. It claims our attention, rather, as an artistic ordering of experience. What a story "means" in an expository sense is simply a part of what it "does." Your understanding of a story should be looked upon as a necessary step toward a full and pleasurable response to its total achievement.

FICTION: THE NOVEL

Since the novel shares many attributes with the short story, most of what you've learned about reading a story can be applied to a novel as well. The primary difference between the two forms is the obvious one: The novel is longer, looser, and more complex.

Instead of a single, relatively simple narrative, a full-length novel often contains a series of *interlocking narratives*. The resolution of one narrative, for instance, may dissolve into the expository stage of the succeeding one. The unity of a novel is thus less rigid than that of a short story. Diverse elements are not excluded, but absorbed.

Many novels therefore exhibit a characteristic *elasticity of form*. The novelist often ignores the strict demands of conventional unity to achieve a goal which the novel alone can approach: a spongelike absorption—within a freely formed artistic unity—of the full and ponderous rhythms of life itself.

In general, the novelist searches not for the best, shortest way to tell his story, but for the best, fullest way.

As a result, novels often contain digressive material, and you may occasionally be justified in skipping or skimming some passages. But this should be done cautiously. Material that at first seems unimportant may later turn out to be vital. You should skip or skim rarely, if at all, in serious works, especially if you desire full understanding.

The interlocking narratives of a novel frequently overlap or blend into one another, and the various elements of a single narrative line may be found in widely separated sections. The exposition and the first signs of increasing tension may appear in an early chapter, and the ultimate resolution of the conflict withheld until the end of the book. Instead of a single sharply focused sequence, the novel presents us with groups of related sequences.

As a literary form, the novel is capable of infinite variety. Such well-known novels as Stephen Crane's *The Red Badge of Courage* and Ernest Hemingway's *The Old Man and the Sea* exhibit the same stringent focus and compression as most short stories. At the other extreme, Tolstoy's *War and Peace* is a classic example of a novel distinguished by fullness, complexity, and a vast number of characters and interlocking narratives. Other novels, especially such twentieth-century examples as James Joyce's *Ulysses* and William Faulkner's *The Sound and the Fury*, derive their complexity not only from their length and fullness but also from their extensive reliance on experimental techniques.

This remarkable diversity makes it difficult to set forth a step-by-step approach that will be of much value, and suggests that the reader must approach this form with an openness and flexibility equal to the writer's. Thus you can make use of the same techniques you learned for the reading of short stories but should be prepared to apply them much more imaginatively, on a much larger scale, and with particular emphasis on the interrelationships between the novel's many narrative and thematic elements.

A novel's theme, for instance, tends to be *inclusive*, serving as a kind of roomy umbrella beneath which the author brings together the many elements of his work. In a sense we can say that a short story's theme tells the writer what he must leave out, whereas a novel's theme tells the writer what he can bring in.

Most novels nonetheless possess a thematic or narrative center which you should be able to discover. In doing this, you needn't be overly concerned about distinguishing the central theme from the various secondary themes, or about your uncertainty in isolating the most important of the several narrative lines. The novel is not a form noted for neatness, and the work itself may not possess the kind of clear-cut demarcation that can be summarized in a simple formulation. Themes and narratives that exist side by side are not always readily distinguishable, and it's possible that two or more of them have equal claim to prominence.

Counterthemes may also be developed, in which one narrative line or set of characters is played off against another for contrast or emphasis. But it's better to have an incomplete, or even somewhat incorrect, idea of a book's central concerns than none at all. A search for coherent patterns at least ensures that you're reading the work actively and alertly and thereby gaining as much understanding as you can.

Since there are so many things a novelist can do, your initial goal should be to find out, at least in general terms, what *kind* of novel you're reading. Is it a realistic portrayal of life at a given time and place? Is it a satire, a fantasy, a re-creation of a historical situation? Does the writer's chief interest appear to be in the actions of his characters, in their psychology, in social conditions, in political or moral issues, in historical or philosophical questions? Is the story presented through the point of view of one or more of the characters, perhaps even in their own language, or is it narrated by the author? Does the novel concentrate on a single extended narrative sequence or does it present a series of related sequences? If it does the latter, which story line seems predominant, and what relationships exist between the various sequences and groups of characters?

In simplest terms, you should find out what the novelist is doing, among the many possible things that he might have done, in order to meet him on his own terms.

You can best accomplish this by again working as much as possible from the general to the particular. In a good novel, each section maintains its own interest and presents its own immediate rewards in terms of enjoyment and understanding. But full comprehension and appreciation require some awareness of the scope and purpose of the whole work.

As with a short story, you should again try to answer the three basic questions pertaining to any narrative: What is happening? Why is it happening? What is its broader significance? In doing this you'll once more be able to employ your knowledge of narrative structure, with particular emphasis on the conflict as the focus of the narrative and the climax as the crucial turning point.

Your approach, though, will have to reflect the fact that a novel is usually composed of a *series* of interlocking narratives. In general, these narratives fall into three categories:

1. The overall sequence
2. Beginning-to-end sequences
3. Self-contained sequences

The overall sequence. This refers to the series of events that produces the main narrative thrust of the work. It generally starts near the beginning of the novel and continues—although often with diversions and interruptions—to build in tension until it finally culminates in a climax and resolution near the end.

In Mark Twain's *Huckleberry Finn*, for example, the overall sequence is the trip down the Mississippi by Huck and the runaway slave, Jim. In everyday terms, the major narrative thrust of a novel is simply what you would say if asked casually by a friend what a book is about. *Huckleberry Finn*, we could say, is about a young boy trying to help a slave escape to freedom by taking a raft down the Mississippi. We should also add, since it's important in establishing the ironic tone and conversational style of the novel, that the story is told in Huck's own words as the first-person narrator.

Beginning-to-end sequences. These story lines also continue pretty much through the whole book, or at least through large sections of it, but are secondary in importance to the overall sequence. In *Huckleberry Finn* there are a series of episodes, clustered around the beginning and the end, dealing with the relationship between Huck and Tom Sawyer. Although Tom doesn't appear in the middle chapters, he is frequently in Huck's thoughts, and the contrast in attitude and behavior between the two boys is clearly established as a continuing element throughout the book.

Several other beginning-to-end sequences function prominently in the work. One deals with the mysterious disappearance of Huck's father and the eventual discovery of his death. Another treats Huck's continuing struggle with his conscience: He's torn again and again between what he's been taught about the "rightness" of slavery and his feelings for Jim as a human being. A third contrasts the oppressiveness of "civilization" ashore with the marvelous sense of freedom Huck enjoys while drifting down the river. There are others, but these examples serve to illustrate the kind of parallel story lines that run through a novel.

Self-contained sequences. These differ from the first two in that they are presented more or less in their entirety at a given point in the book.

Like most novels of some length, *Huckleberry Finn* has many self-contained sequences. Some are no more than minor incidents, while others are quite extensively developed, such as the feud between the Grangerfords and the Shepherdsons, the killing of the loud but harmless drunk, Boggs, by the contemptuous Sherburn, and the escapades dealing with the theatrical performances of the king and the duke.

An awareness of these three types of narratives can lead you to a clearer understanding of the novel's broad-based unity of structure and theme. It can thereby help you avoid a major problem students encounter in reading a novel, which is a tendency to view it as a collection of bits and pieces rather than an organic whole.

Each of these types of sequences can be analyzed in terms of its own narrative structure. Each normally contains exposition, increasing tension, climax, and resolution, and tends to be organized around a central conflict. Normally the overall sequence is the longest and fullest of these story lines, whereas the self-contained sequences exhibit much the same compression and unity as a short story.

In addition to an understanding of these narratives as individual units, you'll want to consider the way in which each contributes to the total effect of the book. The overall sequence should obviously receive the most emphasis, since it can provide valuable clues as to the author's major concerns. It also serves as a center to which you can relate most of the other incidents.

In *Huckleberry Finn*, for instance, the overall sequence dealing with Huck and Jim's flight provides the structural and thematic framework for almost everything that happens. It blends naturally into the sequences showing Huck's battle with his conscience over his role in helping a slave escape, the disappearance and death of Huck's father, Huck's desire to escape from the constraints of "civilization," and the contrasting attitudes of Huck and Tom Sawyer.

It also sets up the basic situation—two runaways continually on the move—that results in the series of separate adventures recounted in the self-contained sequences. These episodes, each with its own narrative structure and its own set of characters, are related in various ways to the overall sequence. The Grangerford-Shepherdson feud, for example, even though it can stand on its own as a complete story, is intertwined on various levels with the book's basic structure and theme. It contributes to the increasing tension of the overall sequence through the dangers that both Huck and Jim are exposed to. It emphasizes the violence and inhumanity of the kind of "civilization" that Huck finds so distasteful. It illustrates the typical feelings toward slavery that Huck struggles with. And although Tom Sawyer does not appear in this section, Huck's honest and unblinking account of the senseless killings reminds us of the contrast between his clear-eyed realism and Tom's boyish romanticism. Finally, we find in this sequence, as we do throughout the book, continuing evidence of the way Twain uses the open-eyed innocence of Huck as narrator to expose the hypocrisy and folly of the society of the day and of human nature in general.

In this way—by looking for connections, parallels, contrasts, and recurring subjects and motifs—your understanding of any part of a book can serve to increase your understanding of all the parts, and of the book as a whole.

The length and complexity of many novels can cause a particular problem for some students. Since they usually read the book in several sittings, they frequently have difficulty carrying over their knowledge from one session to the next. To avoid this, take a few moments to recapitulate in your mind the major events—and whatever you can determine of their narrative and thematic significance—of the section you have just read before you put the book away. You should do the same thing when you come back to the book. These brief summations will help you read more effectively as you go along and allow you to build up a gradually increasing understanding of the book's most important elements. They will also improve your long-range retention of whatever you learn.

Finally, it's necessary to keep in mind once more that you're not trying to reduce a literary form, especially one as wide-ranging as the novel, to a rigid formulation. Your reading should ideally be an experience, and your efforts toward the delineation of narrative patterns and major themes are not ends in themselves. Instead they're valuable, and indeed necessary, steps toward a deep, human response to the book as a creative work.

THE PLAY

The play is a narrative form that shares many attributes with the story and the novel. It also differs from them sharply in some essential ways.

The Play as a Narrative

A play normally employs the same principles of narrative structure as a story and a novel. As a reader, then, you should work toward the same understanding of the writer's major concerns, determining as accurately as you can what happens, why it happens, and its broader significance. And again you can do this by paying particular attention to the crucial elements of conflict, tension, and climax.

A one-act play corresponds roughly in length, unity, and focus to a short story. A full-length play is comparable to a novel in length and complexity and therefore normally contains a series of interlocking narratives and related themes.

The Play as a Performance

Drama differs from fiction in that it is *not* designed primarily to be read. Although many plays are available in printed form, the goal of most dramatists is to have their work performed on a stage. It is this difference that produces the distinctive qualities of drama.

Production Values

A produced play does not depend on words alone for its impact. It also makes vital use of lighting, staging, sound effects, music, sets, and acting. These *production values* are not wholly controlled by the author, since they are largely the responsibility of the director, the stage and lighting designers, and the actors. A skilled dramatist, however, fashions his play so as to take full advantage of these effects. He may, for instance, depend on the lighting and music to help set the mood for a scene, on the movement and expression of an actor to help convey a character's emotions, and on the set to tell the audience a good deal about a character's wealth, status, and background.

When you read a play, however, you have before you only the dialogue, sometimes accompanied by a sketchy description of the characters and settings and a few stage directions—a mere skeleton of the produced work. You have to supply everything else by taking upon yourself the roles of producer, director, designer, and actor. You should therefore try your best to "see" the action as it would occur onstage by visualizing the setting, the characters, and the appropriate movements and gestures. You should also try to "hear" everything that happens, paying particular attention to the way the dialogue would be spoken by the characters, with varying accent, volume, emphasis, and feeling. (In this respect, drama provides an exception, like fiction and poetry in varying degrees, to the desired practice of eliminating auditory responses in your reading.)

Many contemporary dramatists try to help readers by providing much of the information needed for a full response to their work. In his prefatory notes to the reading version of *The Glass Menagerie*, Tennessee Williams comments on "The Music":

> Another extra-literary accent in this play is provided by the use of music. A single recurring tune, "The Glass Menagerie," is used to give emotional emphasis to suitable passages. This tune is like circus music, not when you are on the grounds or in the immediate vicinity of the parade, but when you are at some distance and very likely thinking of something else. It seems under those circumstances to continue almost interminably and it weaves in and out of your preoccupied consciousness; then it is the lightest, most delicate music in the world and perhaps the saddest. It expresses the surface vivacity of life with the underlying strain of immutable and inexpressible sorrow. When you look at a piece of delicately spun glass you think of two things: how beautiful it is and how easily it can be broken. Both of those ideas should be woven into the recurring tune, which dips in and out of the play as if it were carried on a wind that changes. It serves as a thread of connection and allusion between the narrator with his separate point in time and space and the subject of his story. Between each episode it returns as a reference to the emotion, nostalgia, which is the first condition of the play. It is primarily LAURA'S music and therefore comes out most clearly when the play focuses upon her and the lovely fragility of glass which is her image.

As you see, Williams stresses the emotional responses he wishes to evoke, encouraging the reader to employ his own imagination to achieve them.

It's important to remember that many scenic and auditory effects continue throughout a play, as they do in *The Glass Menagerie*, and therefore have to be kept freshly in mind as you read. If a single set is used for the whole play, you should be able to visualize it as clearly in the final scene as in the first. When you read a play in separate sittings, it's helpful to refresh yourself about the physical details as part of the recapitulations that, as with a novel, you should undertake each time you come back. If necessary, you should refer again to the author's stage directions.

Since you probably wouldn't enjoy watching a play in which the actors spoke in a colorless monotone and stood, motionless and indistinguishable, upon an empty stage, you should make every effort to "produce" the play for yourself.

Physical Limitations

In writing for the stage, the playwright accepts certain limitations upon his freedom. Most of these are obvious. Huge casts are out of the question, live animals difficult, and small children a distinct problem. Many types of action cannot be performed on a conventional stage. Sets and scenes cannot be changed at will. And a play of excessive length, or one without intermissions, would have great difficulty being produced.

These are all practical, rather than artistic, matters. They spring from such mundane considerations as the size of the stage, the need to hold down production and operating costs, and the comfort of the audience. Yet a playwright has to work within these constraints to achieve his artistic intent, and this gives his work certain qualities a reader should be familiar with.

For one thing, a good deal of important action often takes place offstage. Sometimes it's because of the nature of the action: automobile crashes, baseball games, long-distance chases, cattle round-ups. On other occasions the playwright is simply trying to conserve valuable minutes or reduce the number of set or scene changes. These offstage happenings are therefore merely reported to us in summary form by the characters. This doesn't mean they're unimportant. In a play, what happens offstage can often be as significant as what happens onstage.

A dramatist also uses special techniques to handle the passage of time. The action of several hours may be compressed into a few minutes of stage time. Without a change of set, or much more than a brief pause in the action, days, months, or years may pass. Long transitions designed only to shift the scene from Saturday night to Monday morning are usually eliminated.

Almost always, the author provides clues as to what he's doing. A dimming of the lights, a change in the background music, a window showing the swift rise of dawn, and a "freeze" of the characters for a few moments are all common devices indicating the passage of time. These are more obvious in the theater than they are in the text, though, and emphasize once more the need to pay close attention to the stage directions.

Practical considerations also dictate that the contemporary author provide at least one intermission, thereby dividing his play into two or possibly three acts. Each develops its own narrative structure, working up to a climactic moment before each curtain. And since the author wants his audience to return after the intermission, these climaxes are designed to produce the tension and suspense that will make them want to do so. A ten- or fifteen-minute intermission is a much more extended break than a blank page in a book, so a dramatist normally provides a much clearer and stronger "hook" between acts than a novelist does between chapters.

A skilled playwright rarely wastes this crucial moment on trivial matters. Therefore the climax of each act can guide you toward a recognition of the author's major themes and the main line of his narrative. It also helps prepare you for what is to come, in that the climax of one act generally provides a new element of tension to be resolved in the next.

Dramatic Compression

Limited as it is in playing time, the contemporary play tends to move forward rapidly, with background exposition held to a minimum. Digressions are rare, and even in relatively complicated plays a dramatist simplifies and compresses as much as possible. As with a short story, you can assume that almost everything in a play forms an integral part of the whole. The structural and thematic elements of a play can therefore generally be stated more precisely than is the case with many novels.

Since theater audiences cannot go back over lines that were not understood the first time, dramatists tend to be more direct in the presentation of important points, and major themes are often stated several times. You should be on the lookout for such statements, especially if they are repeated throughout the play, since they almost always deal with important matters.

As suggested earlier, though, you can't assume that everything of importance will appear specifically in the text. In the imaginative "production" of the play in your mind, you should be prepared to respond to key ideas that may be introduced or reinforced through lighting, sounds, movements, and expressions.

Despite their frequent use of direct statement, playwrights also rely on implication, suggestion, and symbols. In Arthur Miller's *Death of a Salesman*, for instance, Willy Loman exclaims on several occasions that he can't make anything grow in his New York City backyard. Taken in the context of the play, which deals with Willy's personal and professional failures, and especially his frustration in the rearing of his sons, the recurrence of this image suggests a broader meaning. Willy, in truth, has been unable to "make anything grow," to produce in either his own life or his sons' the kind of achievement he yearns for.

The "Absence" of the Author

Finally, we can say that drama is unique among literary forms in that the author cannot speak directly to his audience. In a play, only the characters can speak. The author can give them whatever words he wants but cannot himself say anything.

This leads to what is known as a *spokesman* character. Sometimes, as in Thornton Wilder's *Our Town*, the author uses one of the characters as a clearly identified narrator who fills in the audience on background information and provides a running commentary on the action. More often, the character serving as the author's spokesman is more disguised, playing a role in the action and not separating himself from the other characters by talking directly to the audience.

In *Death of a Salesman* the next-door neighbors, Charley and his son Bernard, serve to question Willy's ideals in a way that probably represents, at least in part, the views of the author. By looking for characters who seem to be presented as decent, reasonable, perceptive individuals, you can often find in what they say and what they stand for a valuable indication of the attitudes of the author.

Reading a play should be no more difficult than reading a short story or novel. Sometimes students find drama more difficult at first because they're less familiar with the form. But if you bring to a play a knowledge of the same narrative and thematic elements you find in fiction and respond alertly to the special qualities of drama, you should be able to read it with considerable understanding and pleasure.

THE POEM

Most people have read prose all their lives and therefore, while exposition, persuasion, fiction, and even drama seem relatively familiar, poetry often strikes them as alien and unapproachable. Of course, poetry *can* be difficult, but the majority of poems are readily accessible to a reader who approaches them with some knowledge of the forms and techniques involved.

Poetry differs from fiction and drama in that it doesn't *have* to present a narrative, and in that it makes greater use of the resources of the language. Poetry relies more heavily on emotional impact than do the other forms, for the poet may not be trying to say anything at all in the normal, expository sense. Instead he may be portraying an emotional state through a series of images or picture-making phrases. He considers himself successful if the results are pure and rich and exact enough to produce the desired impact on the reader, even though it may be difficult for the reader (or the poet) to describe this emotional effect in conventional expository terms.

Suggestion and implication are basic means of expression in poetry, and symbols appear more frequently than in other forms of writing. No matter what a poet is talking about—a rose, a nightingale, a war, a love affair—he is most likely at the same time also talking about something else.

May Sarton, who has written both, compares fiction to a journey and poetry to the arrival. Fiction builds toward a climax through a sequence of events, whereas poetry deals primarily with the climax itself, with a final illumination of some sort, and often does so without buildup, resolution, or exposition. Poetry is not only the most indirect of literary forms but also the most compressed. A poet concentrates on the essence of the subject, on a single flash of recognition or revelation. The reader must discover everything else himself.

Much more than other writers, a poet depends largely for his effect on tone and mood and on his exacting command of the resources of the language. He chooses words both for their precise meaning and for the richness of their connotations. He is very much concerned with the appropriateness of a word's sound, its "color," its accents, its associations, and its visual imagery. "The difference between the right word and the almost-right word," Mark Twain said, "is the difference between lightning and the lighting bug." Even more than other imaginative writers a poet always tries to make lightning strike.

In his poem, "The Second Coming," William Butler Yeats describes a fearful vision of a new kind of prophet returning to the world 2000 years after Christ. He doesn't expect this second Coming to be as hopeful or as exalted as the first. Indeed, Yeats sees the world being visited by a gruesome half-man half-animal. The poem ends with a question as to the identity of this horrendous creature of his vision:

> And what rough beast, its hour come round at last,
> Slouches towards Bethlehem to be born?

"Slouches" is a common enough word, but it is normally used in reference to the way a person stands or sits. Here it describes the way a "rough beast" moves. The image of this creature *slouching* towards its "Bethlehem" jolts the reader in the shocking contrast it suggests between this miracle birth and that of Christ, and implies all manner of ominous forebodings. Trying to think of another verb that could do this better—crawls? moves? slithers? edges? lumbers? creeps?—serves only to convince most readers how vividly Yeats conjures up the overtones he wants by his choice of what seems to be the perfect word.

The Form and Freedom of Poetry

Poetry has been defined as *the tension created between the poet's ideas and the rigid form within which they must be expressed*. The basic characteristics of *poetic form* are:

1. *Rhythm*—a somewhat regular flow of language, based on variations of accents and on lengths of syllables and pauses
2. *Meter*—a more formal rhythmic arrangement based on a relatively unvarying pattern of accents and pauses
3. *Rhyme*—the repetition, usually at regular intervals and at the ends of lines, of words sounding alike
4. *Functional line divisions*—the determination of line length not by mechanical requirements (size of type, width of page, etc.), as in prose, but by the requirements of rhythm, meter, rhyme, phrasing, and content

The *freedom* of poetry springs from many sources. In the first place, the poet has great latitude in the way he accepts, rejects, blends, or varies the elements of poetic form.

The poet is also, as we've said, the only imaginative writer not obliged to use a narrative structure, although of course he can do so if he wishes. Actually, a poet can do almost anything he desires. He can, for instance, write any of the following types of poems, or any combination thereof:

1. *Narrative poem*—one that tells a story

2. *Didactic poem*—one that expounds ideas
3. *Lyric poem*—one that presents personal feelings, usually heightened by emphasis on the "musical" qualities of rhythm, rhyme, and meter, and often meant to be sung
4. *Reflective poem*—one that philosophizes or discusses ideas, often in a discursive manner
5. *Descriptive poem*—one that describes something
6. *Dramatic poem*—one that presents characters primarily through speech, much as a play does, and that may or may not be intended for stage production (*Hamlet,* for instance, can be considered both a play and a long dramatic poem.)

Any of these can be written in a light or serious manner, at whatever length desired (although some feel a lyric poem must be short), on any subject, and for any purpose. A poet can also address his audience directly, or through the thoughts, words, or feelings of one or more created characters. He can invent words and distort the natural construction of phrases and sentences.

In general, you'll find that poems written before the twentieth century depend more heavily on a traditional use of rhyme, meter, stanzaic form, and "poetic" phrasing. Contractions such as "e'er" for "ever" and "o'er" for "over" are common in these earlier works, reflecting the writers' scrupulous concern about formal metrical patterns and the "right" number of syllables and accents in each line. Inverted phrasing, where the words are taken out of their normal order to maintain rhythmic or metrical requirements, also appears frequently in poems written in earlier centuries:

> Avenge O Lord thy slaughter'd Saints, whose bones
> Lie scatter'd on the Alpine Meadows cold,
> Ev'n them who kept thy truth so pure of old.
> John Milton, "On the Late Massacre in Piedmont"

Modern poetry tends to be less formal and less regular in its structure and verbal patterns, and to exhibit a wider variety of both form and content. It may deal with any subject of human concern, from the most elevated to the most base, and may be written in language that is formal, informal, colloquial, or vulgar.

Poetry, said Matthew Arnold, is the "most perfect speech of man." And in his quest for perfection, the poet is free to use any means available, whether traditional or original.

Approaching a Poem

The three basic questions can help you in reading poetry, but since many poems do not have a narrative structure, these questions should be used flexibly.

What is happening? You should first determine what general type of poem you are reading, whether narrative, didactic, lyric, reflective, etc., or a combination of several types. Your purpose is not to "label" the poem, or to restrict your potential responses to it, but simply to develop an initial understanding of the poet's overall approach to his material.

What, for instance, is the basic situation of the poem? In a narrative poem, this can be revealed through the standard narrative elements. For other poems you should figure out who the speaker is, whether it is the poet himself or one or more created characters. What subject, idea, or concern seems to be at the center of the poem? Is the poem related to a specific event, time, or place? Are there characters, real or fictional, in the poem? What do you learn about them? Are there incidents? Is anything important left unstated or implied? Can you figure out what it is?

You should start, in other words, by seeking the *plain sense* meaning of the poem, paying special attention to what appear to be the writer's main concerns. You should normally read a poem several times, gradually soaking up its richness of statement and implication and refining as much as possible your understanding of the work as a whole and of the relationships between its parts. Good poetry is generally too subtle, too compressed, too indirect, and too full of elusive meanings and ambiguities to reveal itself fully on the basis of a single reading. You should be prepared to ponder and study individual words and passages and use dictionaries, encyclopedias, or other reference works as much as you wish. But the overall effect of good poetry springs from the intimate fusion of structure, language, and ideas, so that you should re-read a poem at least several times from beginning to end at a natural pace. A poem should be treated as a unified whole, not just a collection of individual lines.

Ideally, poetry ought to be read aloud, since its sounds and rhythms are a significant part of its total effect. If you cannot do this, you should use the technique of auditory reading to let you "hear" the words in your mind.

Why is it happening? Here again, if you are reading a narrative poem, you can simply follow the approach for other narrative forms.

For poetry in general you can ask yourself various questions. What moves the speaker of the poem to speak? What attitudes does he exhibit toward himself, his subject, his audience? If the speaker is a created character, what attitude does the author reveal, through him, toward the subject of the poem? What has brought about the poem? What has brought about the basic situation of the poem? What is the author's (and, if different the speaker's) attitude toward this situation and its causes?

What is its broader significance? Here you can ask yourself the same questions you asked in reading other forms of imaginative literature. What broader issues of life is the poet writing about? In what way are they reflected in the poem itself? Do the people, events, or situations symbolize or suggest something else? If so, what?

Again, you should be careful not to overinterpret. You should also remember that, important as it is to understand a poem, poetry is intended not merely to be understood but to be *absorbed*. You will find that the broader significance of poetry is not always easily discovered or simply phrased. But if a poem has an effect on you, if you are moved by it, or if you have an emotional (even if not an intellectual) awareness of what the poet is saying, your reading can probably be considered successful.

Practice in Reading Poems

We can now look at a few poems in order to suggest some of the ways in which an alert reader might respond to them.

JUDGEMENTS
William Stafford

I accuse—
   Ellen: you have become forty years old,
   and successful, tall, well-groomed,
   gracious, thoughtful, a secretary.
   Ellen, I accuse.
George—
   You know how to help others;
   you manage a school. You never
   let fear or pride or faltering plans
   break your control.
   George, I accuse.
I accuse—
   Tom: you have found a role;
   now you meet all kinds of people
   and let them find the truth of your
   eminence; you need not push.
   Oh, Tom, I do accuse.
Remember—
   The gawky, hardly to survive students
   we were: not one of us going to succeed,
   all of us abjectly aware of how cold,
   unmanageable the real world was?
   I remember. And that fear was true.
   And is true.
Last I accuse—
   Myself: my terrible poise, knowing
   even this, knowing that then we
   sprawled in the world
   and were ourselves part of it; now
   we hold it firmly away with gracious
   gestures (like this of mine!) we've achieved.
   I see it all too well—
   And I am accused, and I accuse.

The surface of this poem is straightforward, and the tone conversational. The speaker expresses himself quite directly, and there are no spectacular effects. The poem's effectiveness results, on the contrary, from its restraint, precision, and compression, and from the depth of feeling conveyed about people who are made to seem very real to us.

The first three stanzas present a startling contrast between the flat accusations and the list of the "sins" referred to, which actually sounds like a catalog of virtues: "successful," "gracious," "thoughtful," "you know how to help others," "you need not push."

The first and second stanzas end similarly: "Ellen, I accuse" and "George, I accuse." In the third stanza this refrain is changed to "Oh, Tom, I do accuse." The break in the pattern signals a shift in the structure of the poem from the accusations themselves to the reminiscences of the fourth stanza. It also introduces a new tone, almost like a break in the voice of the speaker. He has been condemning these people, we realize, not in anger but in sadness and regret.

The fourth stanza reveals his relationship to the three people named: They were all "hardly to survive" students together, not one of whom was "going to succeed." Yet as we've seen from the early stanzas, all three did succeed. Why, then, is the speaker disappointed in them?

The fifth stanza tells us. It does something else too, in that the speaker here turns his criticism upon himself. He, too, he confesses, has achieved a kind of success which dismays him. As students they were "sprawled in the world and were ourselves part of it." Now, though, they hold the world "firmly away with gracious gestures (like this of mine!)."

The poem ends quietly, with a simple but moving restatement: "And I am accused, and I accuse."

Brief, uncluttered, and without any of the pretentious or flamboyant phrasing people sometimes consider "poetic," the poem illustrates how a good writer can achieve his effects with simplicity and grace. The natural phrasing hardly calls attention to itself, yet it would be difficult to improve upon. "*Sprawled* in the world" shows how even a familiar word can be used freshly, creating as it does a richly suggestive image of the sort of carelessness, the youthful lack of concern with appearance, decorum, and ambition, that the speaker and his friends exemplified as students.

In the preceding stanza, "gawky" and "unmanageable" do much the same thing, describing the characters as students and at the same time suggesting a whole way of life that contrasts revealingly with the terms used to describe their success ("well-groomed, gracious").

Throughout, the speaker's "flat" style also serves to emphasize his sincerity and honesty, and his willingness to face uncomfortable truths, even about himself, without resorting to evasion or exaggeration.

It should also be noted how effectively, in a few lines, Stafford has characterized four people at two widely separated times of their lives and has made us share his disappointment over the way their lives have turned out. It's a subject complex enough for a novel. The poem, though, does not aim for fullness, for narrative development. Its virtues are economy, precision, freshness, and suggestion. Stafford creates the effect he wants through a skillful selection of illuminating insights and exact perceptions.

Perhaps we could say that the broader significance of the poem lies in the universality of the accusations made against the characters. They've achieved, we realize, a superficial success that has robbed them of their vitality and submerged their humanity beneath "gracious gestures." Stafford seems to be writing about the loss of youth, energy, fire, and naturalness, all in the pursuit of success.

The poem therefore presents a picture of what happens, or can happen, to certain people. But the real achievement is perhaps the suggestion that the reader, like the speaker, is not immune to these accusations. To the young reader, Stafford warns of what might happen. To the older reader he presents, in sadness more than bitterness, a picture that all too many will recognize as a portrait of their friends, and themselves.

SAVAGE
Michael S. Harper

The savage broke the walls out
and bulled into the wilderness.
We sat recalling his unspeakable
ingratitude, of our equipment,
the time we'd lose,
the experiment not yet done.

Brief as it is, Harper's poem implies with its few details a complete narrative. The "savage" and "we" are the characters in conflict. The narrator and his colleagues cannot understand why their captive would want to escape from their control. They obviously are convinced that their "experiment" is worthwhile and are angered by what they see as their subject's selfishness in breaking loose, his lack of concern over the inconvenience and disruption he has caused them.

In Stafford's poem the speaker was presented sympathetically, as a person of understanding and deep human feelings. Harper seems to be doing just the opposite—giving us a speaker who is selfish, unfeeling, narrow-minded, and without compassion. The speaker therefore seems to express a point of view that the poet wishes to expose and condemn.

What is really happening in the poem, though? What kind of experiment were these people trying to carry out? What sort of equipment is referred to? We're not told; nor are we given a specific setting or time for the incident. We have to assume, therefore, that the poet is primarily interested not in the details of a single incident but rather in the basic human and historical issues suggested by it. Would it make a difference in the poem's effect, for instance, if the time were the present or the past? The captive an American Indian, a Samoan, a Vietnamese, a Nigerian? The experimenters Americans, Englishmen, Belgians, Frenchmen, Japanese, Russians?

The poem applies to almost any combination of these elements. Harper seems to be writing about the colonialist attitude of the "haves" and its effects on the "have-nots" of the world. By not restricting the incident to a specific time or place he encourages the reader to consider all the situations to which it could apply, whenever, in other words, representatives of technologically advanced societies intrude upon the members of an "underdeveloped" culture and treat them as little more than laboratory animals.

Through the words of the narrator, Harper exposes an attitude he considers immoral and antihuman in the expectation that the reader will reject it. Not only is the speaker shown to be arrogant toward the subjects of his experiment, and by extension toward their whole history and culture, but as pompously self-righteous to boot. He remains oblivious to the feelings and rights of his captive and is concerned only about such "important" matters as the time that will be lost, the expense of his equipment, and the necessity of his experiment. Surely the use of the title "Savage" is ironic. Who, Harper asks by implication, is the real "savage" in this situation?

The relative ease with which the poem makes this point, and the broad areas of history it encompasses in the precise rendering of a single incident, indicate how a skilled poet can make a virtue out of compression. It is not simply that he tells a story in a very few words. It is that the story he tells touches a nerve and activates a whole network of responses. He gives us all we need to know—can you think of anything that ought to be added?—and leaves us to our own responses. He doesn't tell us what we should think or how we should feel. The poet, in this case, says nothing, because the poem has said everything.

CITY ROSES
(Want some fun, baby?)
George Barlow

Blooming patiently
in every corner
of this nervous garden,
these roses spread
their petals
for bumblebees
to come in
and leave their pollen;
green, folded,
tucked away for safety
in half-hidden blossoms.
A blackbird sings blues
from the juke box
in a hot links joint nearby.
Scooby cruises
through his garden
and whispers to a rose:
"Turn a lotta sunshine, baby!
Take in plenty pollen,
sweet-fine-thang!"

Barlow's poem, like the first two we looked at, presents a carefully selected series of details which only gradually reveal their unity. But there are suggestions here, right from the beginning, of certain unexplained or contradictory elements which need to be dealt with.

Most readers will have little difficulty discovering what the poem seems to be about. Taking the title literally, we can read this as a portrait of a man, Scooby, who enthusiastically nourishes a small rose garden in some unnamed city. We can easily envision his "nervous garden" crowded between buildings in the urban hubbub, with a "juke box in a hot links joint nearby." The poem ends with Scooby urging his flowers to grow and flourish. From his word choice and pronunciation ("sweet-fine-thang!") we can assume he's probably black.

All this seems relatively obvious. But all along we've emphasized that a good poem is tightly unified, with every word contributing to the total effect. If this is true of Barlow's poem, we should reconsider some of the elements that don't seem to fit into our interpretation.

We could begin with the parenthetical subtitle —"Want some fun, baby?" It could be argued that it refers to Scooby's enjoyment of gardening, but the tone seems wrong for that. And who is "baby"? Possibly one of the flowers, since at the end of the poem Scooby also addresses a rose in this way. If the phrase refers to Scooby's fun, though, it doesn't seem likely that he would invite one of the flowers to join him in it. Since the subtitle is so prominent, we expect it to be significant, yet it's hard at first to see how it adds anything to the poem.

There are also discordant elements within the body of the poem, again suggesting the possibility that our initial interpretation may have to be revised. The pollen left by the bumblebees is described as "green, folded." The use of "green" could be taken as a kind of poetic license, since the color is generally suggestive of natural growth and fertility. "Folded," though, presents a real problem. It's hard to visualize pollen as being folded or to imagine why the poet uses this word. What is suggested by it? How does it contribute to the image of a city garden?

Then we're told that this "green, folded" pollen is "tucked away for safety." Again, the first part of the image might work, although "tucked" leaves us a bit doubtful. "For safety," however, hardly seems to function at all within the garden setting.

A closer look at the next passage may give us some help in dealing with our puzzlement:

A blackbird sings blues
from the juke box
in a hot links joint nearby.

The blackbird could be accepted as an actual bird, singing "blues" because it is just as much out of its element in the city as the garden is. At the same time, we could read this passage quite differently. A "bird" in music parlance is a female band singer. Perhaps what we have is a *black bird*, a black vocalist singing blues on a record in the nearby bar. This also fits in with our general interpretation—the singer emerging as another of the "city" images contrasting with the "natural" image of the garden.

Since both readings of this passage work equally well, we could take this as a sign that the poet uses this technique throughout, suggesting alternative but more-or-less consistent interpretations. If so, what sort of second level of meaning can explain the details that don't fit into the first? As always, we should take care to work from the text itself and not to distort the poem through wild guesses.

Let's return to the "green, folded" pollen. If we put aside the garden imagery for a moment, the words seems to suggest money—green, folded bills. Does "pollen" also support this? Perhaps, since pollen is an enriching ingredient in the flowering process and is necessary for fertilization. Webster's *New World Dictionary* defines pollen as the "powderlike male sex cells on the stamen of a flower."

The passage thus introduces two elements, money and sex, that we didn't see in the poem earlier. The question of course is whether they really belong.

The parenthetical subtitle suggests they might. "Want some fun, baby?" has long been known as a phrase used by prostitutes, especially streetwalkers in large cities, in soliciting business. This reinforces the tentative themes of money and sex we've set up and so can't be dismissed out of hand.

In fact, if we look at the last three lines again, Scooby tells the rose to "Take in plenty pollen." This supports the use of pollen as money, and the reference to prostitution. He also urges the flower to "Turn a lotta sunshine." "Turn" seems to be an odd word here until we realize that it too is commonly used among prostitutes; to "turn a trick" is to perform sex for money.

At this point we have enough encouragement to test our second interpretation against the poem as a whole.

It holds up well through the first three lines. And the succeeding passage, in which the roses "spread their petals for bumblebees to come in and leave their pollen," seems obviously sexual. And if the pollen is both male sex cells and money, the prostitution motif is strongly reinforced. It's further supported by the bills being "tucked away for safety in half-hidden blossoms," especially with the similarity in sound between "blossoms" and "bosoms." We can easily visualize the prostitute taking money from a client and tucking it safely into the bodice of her dress.

We're then brought back to Scooby, who whispers encouragement to his roses in a manner that, as we have already noted, is consistent both in phrasing and content with the world of prostitution. If that's the world Barlow is writing about, Scooby's role is clearly that of a pimp, encouraging his girls to turn a lot of tricks and taken in plenty of money. It could also be noted that the rose has a long history of use by poets and writers as a symbol of the female sex organs. Thus "Scooby cruises through his garden" in the poem, and in our imaginations, as a chilling portrait of a "gardener" who nurtures human "roses" for his own greed.

Nothing in the poem seems to contradict this interpretation, which not only eliminates our earlier difficulties but also gives us a way of responding to the poem that represents it as a coherent and consistent whole. What Barlow has done, it now seems evident, is to develop his theme on two levels at the same time. Our first reading, in other words, was not "wrong." It was simply incomplete, pertaining only to the first and more obvious contrast between the natural and the artificial, as seen in the image of roses blooming in the "nervous garden" of an overcrowded city. At the same time, as the inconsistencies of this reading indicated, he also presents a second embodiment of the same theme. The young girls in Scooby's brothel are as much a part of nature as roses, perhaps even as beautiful, but the natural human activity of lovemaking has been corrupted for them into little more than a way of making money, of staying alive in the city's hostile and unnatural environment.

These three poems shouldn't be considered typical of the sort you may be reading. Every poem, if it succeeds, does so uniquely. We've simply tried to illustrate some of the ways poets work, some of the effects they try to achieve, and some of the difficulties, and rewards, that they offer. Most of all, though, we've tried to show that most poetry *is* accessible to an interested reader who's willing to respond fully and perceptively. A good poem needs a good reader, and deserves one. With a little effort, what now perhaps seems difficult can soon turn into something immensely rewarding and stimulating.

The poet Charles Simic ends one of his works with these lines:

This is a tale with a kernel.
You'll have to use your own teeth to crack it.

He speaks here for all poets and to all readers.

Chapter 10

Writing about Literature

The practical value of writing about literature is not really as obscure as students sometimes feel. It encourages you to sharpen your perceptions, organize your thinking, and improve your writing.

There is a common objection based on a misconception—the theory of blissful ignorance—which contends that the less you know about something, the more you will enjoy it. The truth is that writing about literature doesn't take the fun out of it any more than talking about it or thinking about it. It should be noted that people who fear some great loss of pleasure if they learn anything about literature rarely apply this theory to other pastimes. Does the fan who's mastered the strategy and rules of baseball enjoy it less than someone who's ignorant of these fine points? Can you really get much excitement out of the game if you don't know what the purpose of a bunt is?

In writing about literature, you'll be encouraged to excel in two vital skills: reading and writing. You'll be asked to react coherently to stimuli—works of literature—that are not cut and dried, that are as complex and various as life itself. You'll have to come to grips with the work and also, perhaps more importantly, with your own attitudes and perceptions. You'll have to make your reactions clear to yourself and then make them clear to a reader.

Neither of these tasks is easy, but neither is as difficult as many assume. In the previous chapter we discussed the first task, learning to deal effectively with a variety of literary works. In this chapter we'll suggest ways to communicate your reactions to a reader.

Some General Guides

Use What You've Learned

Your work in the preceding chapter can serve as a starting point. To write about a novel, a play, or a poem, you have to begin with a thorough understanding of the work itself. There is no way around this. You'll also be able to make use of everything you've learned about the writing of exposition and persuasion. The qualities of good writing discussed in earlier chapters will serve you just as well here.

Writing about literature is not the exotic undertaking that it may seem to be. You'll simply be asked to read as you've learned to read and write as you've learned to write. The only difference is that you'll be writing about literary subjects.

Work at Your Own Level

You can avoid a good many potential problems by being realistic in choosing and developing your subjects. Don't aim beyond your capabilities and don't try to sound like a literary critic. Essays dealing with literary subjects seem particularly susceptible to pretentious writing. Some students feel they have to sound "literary," and struggle to maintain a pose of intellectual sophistication.

If you haven't had much experience in analyzing literary works, don't pretend that you have. If you haven't worked much with poetry, for example, try to avoid topics that require an intimate knowledge of the complexities of meter and rhythm. If you're asked to write about a novel that you've found particularly difficult, choose a subject dealing with the more manageable aspects of character or story rather than the subtleties of tone or point of view.

This is not to say that challenging subjects will remain forever beyond your reach. Learning in any field is a gradual process, and no one starts out as an expert. Both your reading and your writing will improve with practice, but you'll always do best by not pretending to an expertise that you've not yet achieved.

THREE KINDS OF LITERARY ESSAYS

To help you respond more confidently to these assignments, we'll discuss the three types of papers you'll most likely be asked to write, and suggest appropriate topics for each.

The three most common types of literary essays written in college are:

1. The intensive study
2. The comparison
3. The research paper

As we'll see, these categories overlap in some respects, but they're distinctive enough to provide helpful guidelines. It should also be noted that all three can be written with varying degrees of personal involvement. Each, for instance, can provide the basis for *pure exposition,* or for either type of persuasive writing—the *factual presentation* or the *personal opinion* paper.

Initially, we'll assume that you're writing purely expository papers in which your purpose is simply to *inform* the reader through an objective report on the work under consideration, without extensive interpretation or analysis. The emphasis should be on the literary work, not on your reactions to it.

Absolute objectivity is of course unattainable when a human being confronts a work of literature. You are not a machine, and a book is not an equation. Your intelligence and judgment necessarily play a large part in deciding what to include and what to emphasize. You also have to exercise critical discretion in discovering the central narrative and thematic concerns. And any account of the book's broader significance, especially if it is only implied by the author, often requires a good deal of personal interpretation.

After we've discussed these three types of papers as straightforward exposition, we'll indicate how they can also serve as the basis for persuasive papers.

The Intensive Study

The sort of "book report" assignment frequently given in high school, designed to present a general summary of a literary work, is rarely used in college. Instead of trying to cover everything about a literary work, you are almost always expected to concentrate on a more limited subject and to give a more detailed presentation. Normally you should focus on either a single section or aspect of a work.

The *section* could be a scene from a play, a chapter or incident from a novel, or a passage from a poem:

> Developing Suspense: The Opening Sections of Charles G. Finney's *The Circus of Dr. Lao*
>
> The Collapse of Ambition: The Final Scenes of Shakespeare's *Macbeth*
>
> The Women in the Pub: An Analysis of a Section of T. S. Eliot's Poem, "The Wasteland"

You can refer in your paper to other sections of the work, or to its overall concerns, and in general can introduce whatever material seems appropriate. But your main focus should be on a specific part of the work, and there's no obligation to treat the rest of the work in any detail.

Note that the first example has a double limitation. It not only focuses on the opening passages of a novel but also upon a particular aspect—the suspense—relating to that part of the book. The same is true of the Macbeth topic, where a single section of the play and a single idea—the collapse of ambition—both serve to limit the paper.

When asked to limit your paper to a single *aspect* of a work, your topic would typically be of this nature:

> Hemingway's attitude toward duty in *A Farewell to Arms*
>
> Growth and Decay in Theodore Roethke's Greenhouse Poems
>
> The Role of the Gentleman Caller in Tennessee Williams' *The Glass Menagerie*

However the topic is narrowed, you will be expected to deal with it *intensively,* through a close reading of the text. And of course you'll need a good understanding of the whole work before you'll be able to write intelligently about your more limited topic.

Unless your topic is extremely narrow—covering perhaps a few lines of a poem—it's important in developing your papers to make use of the principles of *selection* and *emphasis*. Concentrate on the details that seem most important to the work and most appropriate to your topic.

You can best achieve a meaningful selection by making use of the knowledge gained in Chapter 9, "Reading Imaginative Literature." In dealing with a narrative form, for instance, you'll probably want to address the three basic questions:

1. What is happening?
2. Why is it happening?
3. What is its broader significance?

These answers should illuminate the central conflict of the work, the opposing forces, the climax, and the resolution.

In dealing with a poem that lacks a narrative structure, you'll similarly want to make sure you understand the basic situation of the poem—the speaker, the theme, the central images, the tone, and the attitudes of the poet.

It's also helpful to remember the value of *concrete illustrations*. You'll find it difficult to present an effective report on your close reading in vague terms and should make liberal use of supporting details and specific examples. Character names and relationships, place names, significant dates, and specific events indicate a surer grasp of the material than a collection of vague generalizations.

Consider the following sentence from a paper on Hemingway's *A Farewell to Arms*:

> The main character and his girlfriend finally get fed up with the way things are going and decide to run away together.

This statement is true but is too fuzzy to tell the reader much. Nor does it indicate a precise knowledge of the book. It could be more effectively stated as follows:

> Lieutenant Henry becomes disillusioned with the war in Italy, especially the disorganization and futility of the Allied effort, and deserts to neutral Switzerland with Catherine Barkley, the English nurse he loves.

The second version is somewhat longer, but the length is justified by improved clarity and concreteness.

If you were writing about the way Charles Finney develops suspense at the beginning of *The Circus of Dr. Lao*, you could start by making a rough list of points that might be included, based on your close study of this aspect of the novel:

1. Advertisement for the circus
   a. Provocative phrasing
   b. Mystery as to who placed the advertisement
   c. Claim for "animals no man had ever seen before"
2. Circus parade
   a. Only "three frowsy beast-drawn wagons"
   b. Horse or unicorn?
   c. The "green dog"
3. Reactions of townspeople
   a. Newspaperman (Mr. Etaoin)
   b. Lawyer, widow, college youth, etc.

Each of these points could be specifically developed as an illustration of the way in which the author creates suspense. They wouldn't necessarily be presented in the order listed of course, and some thought would have to be given to their relative importance. But they could provide the basis for a successful expository paper on this topic, in that they would serve to inform the reader in concrete terms of the precise manner in which the author creates a suspenseful opening for his novel.

The Comparison

You're probably familiar with this sort of paper, as it lends itself to assignments in many fields. It's also widely used with literary subjects. Two or more works, or parts of works, are discussed in relation to their similarities and differences. Although any piece of literature can conceivably be compared with any other, normally works are chosen that are similiar enough to justify their being considered together.

They might, for instance, share the same subject. Both James Tate's "The Lost Pilot" and Randall Jarrell's "The Death of the Ball Gun Turret Gunner" are about a World War II airman killed in action. Tate's poem is very personal, based on the death of the poet's father, while Jarrell's poem, which doesn't reveal any relationship between poet and subject, is more objective in tone and more factual.

There are other differences that could also be explored: in style, level of reality, imagery and metaphor, tone, use of irony, etc. In each case, though, the paper would proceed from a rather obvious similarity to a discussion of more subtle differences. The approach would therefore allow us to learn more about both poems, and both poets, by discovering their divergent ways of exploring the same subject.

The following pairings of novels could also serve well to illustrate different ways of handling similiar material:

> The athlete as hero: Bernard Malamud's *The Natural*, and Mark Harris' *Bang the Drum Slowly*
>
> The American Businessman: Sinclair Lewis' *Babbitt*, and William Dean Howell's *The Rise of Silas Lapham*

Even works that seem quite different on the surface often possess similarities which are not obvious at first glance. Robert Frost's "The Hill Wife" is a relatively brief poem, whereas Gustav Flaubert's *Madame Bovary* is a long, detailed novel. Beyond their obvious differences in form and technique, however, both portray a wife in revolt against an oppressive marriage. A paper could therefore use these works to illustrate the distinctive characteristics of poetry and fiction, as well as to explore the varying attitudes of the authors and the characters.

A comparison could also be based on cultural or chronological differences. Robert Burns "O My Love's Like a Red, Red Rose" is a short poem written by a Scotsman in the 1790s. William Carlos Williams' *Asphodel, That Greeny Flower* is a long poem written by an American in the 1950s. Both, however, are love poems and could be discussed together in reference to any number of points, including style, form, length, and complexity. They could also provide the basis for an exploration of the attitudes of each author, and of the differing personal, social, and historical forces that may have helped shape them.

You can thus approach a comparison paper either by starting with the similarities and analyzing the differences, or vice versa. You should bear in mind, though, that the end product should be something more than a kind of "laundry list" of similarities and differences. You'll be expected, in other words, to select your material judiciously and to develop your points fully enough to illuminate significant aspects of the works being discussed.

A comparison paper differs from the other two types of literary essays only in that it deals with more than one work. The comparisons made therefore normally reflect the close study of individual sections and aspects exemplified by an *intensive study*. A comparison can also be used as the basis of the third type, the *research paper*, which we look at now.

The Research Paper

This type of paper differs from the others in that your study of the literary works is supplemented by additional outside reading. The kind of additional material used depends largely on the nature of your subject.

Thus the research could deal with *biographical information*:

> Hawthorne's Experience at Brook Farm as a Source, for *The Blithesdale Romance*

or *literary sources* and influences:

> The Colloquial Style: Gertrude Stein's Theories and Sherwood Anderson's Practices

or *critical writings*:

> The "Rediscovery" of Henry James: Critical Reactions from 1900 to 1920
> Poe's Reputation among European Critics
> The Last Chapter of Stephen Crane's *The Red Badge of Courage*: Some Differing Interpretations

or *public reaction*:

> The Effect of Upton Sinclair's *The Jungle* on Pure Food Legislation
> The Popularity of the Detective Story

In each instance you should begin by gaining a thorough understanding of the literary works themselves and then proceed to your investigation of the appropriate outside sources. The research portion of the project requires an ability to use the library effectively and to gather information in an organized manner. For a formal paper, you would also be expected to document your sources through footnotes and a bibliography. If you are not familiar with such practices, you should again probably refer to an appropriate guide, such as Elinor Yaggy's *How to Write Your Term Paper*.

The unique feature of the research paper is this use of additional material. In other ways it generally assumes the form of either an intensive study or a comparison paper. In each case, the procedure is the same as that outlined earlier, except for the additional use of outside material.

WRITING PERSUASIVE PAPERS ABOUT LITERATURE

As mentioned earlier, each of the three types of literary essays can exhibit different levels of personal involvement. To simplify our discussion of these types, we've so far assumed that in each case you are writing a purely expository paper. The degree of personal involvement expected of you will usually be indicated by the instructor, and it's important that you have a clear understanding of this part of the assignment.

There are thus two ways in which you can define the nature of your paper. You should first of all determine which of the three types of essays, or what combination of them, you are being asked to write:

1. The intensive study
2. The comparison
3. The research paper

You can then decide what degree of involvement is called for. You may be asked to write:

1. Pure exposition
2. Persuasion (factual presentation)
3. Persuasion (personal opinion)

Not all instructors use the same terminology, so it is up to you to make sure you understand both the general scope and format of the assignment and the degree of personal involvement required.

Pure Exposition

If you're asked to write an objective report on your reading, in which you deal exclusively with the style, content, or attitudes of the author, you should consider it an exercise in *expository* writing. You can then proceed according to the general guidelines we've suggested for an expository treatment of any of the three types of literary essays.

You should have no added difficulty writing about literature in a *persuasive* manner, since the basic principles set forth in Chapter 8, "Writing Persuasion," can serve as an overall guide, along with the knowledge you have gained about the distinctive features of the intensive study, the comparison, and the research paper.

Persuasion (Factual Presentation)

If you're instructed to present an analysis or interpretation of a literary work, you're probably being asked to write a persuasive paper of the kind we defined as a *factual presentation*. This requires you to present the "facts" in an impartial manner and then to draw logical conclusions from them. As applied to a literary essay, this means that you should set forth your account of what you've read much as you would for an expository paper, but that you shouldn't stop there. You must then use this material as the basis for a reasonable and well-supported analysis.

For the topic "Hemingway's attitude toward duty" you would therefore have a twofold objective. Your first responsibility would be the same as for an expository paper—to present an accurate account of the way the author deals with this concept in *A Farewell to Arms*. You would then be expected to evaluate this material in order to arrive at a well-supported conclusion that represents a fair statement of Hemingway's attitude.

In some cases, the author states his ideas directly and clearly. More often, they are only implied or suggested, and it is up to you to weigh both the specific details and the general implications of the work in order to set forth your conclusion.

Your own judgments and your own interpretations will thus clearly influence the paper, and they should, since you're engaged in persuasive writing. But your conclusions shouldn't merely represent generalized *feelings*. They ought to be solidly grounded in specific references to the book itself. In essence, the paper should not so much reflect *your* concerns as it should make a persuasive case for what you see as the author's concerns.

Even though a factual presentation paper thus requires a good deal of analysis by you, the focus remains clearly on the literary work and on your conclusions based on a perceptive reading of the author's words.

Persuasion (Personal Opinion)

If you're asked to use your reading of a literary work as the basis for an expression of your own attitudes, beliefs, and reactions, you are being assigned what we've defined as a *personal opinion* paper.

Here the emphasis shifts from the work itself to your opinions about it. This is not of course meant to encourage careless or superficial reading. For your opinions to influence an intelligent reader they obviously have to be based on a clear understanding of the work you've read.

But you *are* being asked to express your own ideas and should be prepared to do so. For the Hemingway paper, therefore, your goal now becomes threefold:

First, to present a fair and accurate recounting of the development of the theme of duty in *A Farewell to Arms*, as you would for an expository paper. Then, to use your own critical judgment to describe Hemingway's attitude toward duty, as you would for a persuasive paper based on a factual presentation. Finally, to make this a personal opinion paper by evaluating Hemingway's concepts of duty on the basis of *your* attitudes and opinions.

The paper will not be judged merely as a presentation of your own ideas, as would a personal essay on "my concept of duty." You have to remember that you're writing about literature, and that your attitudes should serve as a means of evaluating someone else's—in this case a novelist's—as they are embodied in a literary work.

You may, for instance, question, agree with, or disagree with, Hemingway's concepts in various ways. Do you feel his ideas of duty are romanticized and unrealistic? Would they lead to unquestioning subservience of the individual to authority? Do you feel they are applicable only to wartime or other emergency situations and are unacceptable in normal life? Does Hemingway's presentation of the reasons for Lieutenant Henry's desertion support the author's general attitude toward duty, or does he introduce a new element, that of duty to oneself or to some higher form of morality? How does one decide when duty to a higher morality supercedes one's duty to organizations, causes, governments, or friends and associates? If everyone were to exercise the right to act on the basis of a personal definition of "duty," would this lead to chaos or to a more moral and perhaps more peaceful world?

As with all personal opinion papers, your purpose is not to find the "right" answer. The topic chosen is to be explored, considered, and delved into.

Almost any substantial work of literature offers a wide choice of potential subjects for a personal opinon paper. The paper, though, should always tell the reader a good deal about both the author's ideas *and* your own. If the author's are delineated fairly and yours are developed convincingly, you will have the basis for a good personal opinion paper.

Writing about Different Literary Forms

All three types of literary essays, whatever level of emotional involvement they reflect, can be used —as our examples have shown—to discuss stories, novels, plays, or poems.

Each literary form, however, possesses unique qualities, and it might be helpful now to consider writing about literature from the viewpoint of the special attributes of fiction, drama, and poetry. Certain subjects, for instance, are appropriate to all forms, while others have a more limited application.

The lists that follow are not intended to be complete or to limit you in any way. But students often have trouble thinking of topics to write about, and you may want to refer to a list of possibilities arranged according to literary form.

It should be noted that these are subject *areas*, not topics. Each of these broad areas can yield numerous specific topics, and you should make sure that your topic is sufficiently limited to serve as the basis for a successful paper. Part of the narrowing-down process naturally entails a decision as to which of the types of literary essays, and what degree of personal involvement, seem appropriate for your assignment.

Subject Areas for Narrative Forms (Story, Novel, Play) and for Many Poems
1. Characters
2. Narrative structure (including setting, exposition, conflict, climax, resolution, etc.)
3. Themes (the central concerns of the author)
4. Literary technique (suspense, dialogue, methods of characterization, mood, descriptions, setting, point of view, diction, symbolism, credibility, stylistic qualities, etc.)
5. Level of reality (realism, fantasy, melodrama, etc.)
6. Overall tone (comic, tragic, satiric, etc.)
7. Philosophical or moral concerns
8. Social or political issues
9. Biographical, literary, or historical background
10. Critical reactions and evaluations
11. Interrelationship between elements (between characters and theme, tone and subject, style and political ideas, the author's life and his work, etc.; also between major and minor characters, narrative sequences, themes, etc.)

Additional Subject Areas for Plays
1. Dramatic conventions (stage effects, offstage action, etc.)
2. Spokesman characters
3. Settings
4. The division into acts and scenes
5. Dramatic compression (techniques for summarizing action, indicating the passage of time, presenting exposition, etc.)

Additional Subject Areas for Poems
1. Poetic techniques (rhyme, rhythm, meter, line breaks, etc.)
2. Language (symbols, imagery, metaphors, diction, tone, mood, formal or informal usage, implied statements, irony, etc.)
3. The general situation (time, place, setting, implied or stated background, etc.)
4. The speaker (relationship to author, to reader, to real or imaginary audience, etc.)
5. Structure and form (conventional, free, experimental)
6. Allusions to literature, myth, or history
7. Type of poem (dramatic, didactic, lyric, narrative, etc.)

Writing about Literature: Some Final Suggestions

We began this chapter by saying that papers on literary topics are not really as difficult, nor as exotic, as many students imagine. Having indicated the types of papers you can write and the kinds of topics you can deal with, we conclude by emphasizing the principles underlying this approach:

1. *Know what is expected of you.* It's much easier and more effective to begin with a clear idea of the type of paper that has been assigned, and the level of personal involvement expected.
2. *Read as you've learned to read.* The techniques of active and alert reading, and your knowledge of the various forms of literature, should be employed to gain full command over the work being discussed.
3. *Write as you've learned to write.* The attributes of good writing apply to papers dealing with literary subjects, and you shouldn't strain for an artificially "intellectual" style. Good organization, a clear and compressed style, and an acceptable level of mechanical correctness are still the basic characteristics of a successful essay.
4. *Choose subjects that reflect your abilities.* As much as possible, try to pick topics and treatments that are appropriate to your natural interests and to your experience in dealing with literary subjects.
5. *Use concrete examples to illustrate and support your points.* Avoid vague and sweeping generalizations through the use of specific references to the work you're discussing. The citation of names, places, and events not only strengthens your writing but also indicates a detailed knowledge of your subject.
6. *State your ideas reasonably.* Bear in mind that you're dealing with works of literature which are susceptible to numerous interpretations and can be approached from many points of view. Final answers are rare, and even the wisest of critics have their blind spots. A certain amount of modesty in setting forth your interpretations is therefore advisable. Don't hesitate to exercise your critical judgment or to express your opinions when they're called for, but do so with restraint, aware of the possibility that you may have misread or overlooked something or may have been unduly influenced by certain preconceptions. Your purpose is not to reveal some final and unalterable truth. Rather it's to make a thoughtful and honest attempt to explore some of the qualities of fiction, drama, and poetry that have continued over the ages to engage our interest and emotions.

Chapter 11

Remembering What You Read: Studying and Test Taking

The skills involved in studying and test taking are obviously related. You have to study well if you are to perform well in a test. Yet even your best efforts at studying will be of no avail if you can't reproduce your knowledge under examination conditions. It is important therefore to work for improvement in both areas.

STUDYING

Like reading, studying is a vital skill that receives less attention than it merits. Few students, therefore, study as efficiently as they might. To study well, you must have good memory habits, take useful notes, and learn well from these notes. This is true for all subjects. Each requires you to master a different kind of material, but the principles remain the same whether you're memorizing formulas, trying to understand relationships, or preparing to evaluate abstract concepts.

Developing Good Memory Habits

Whether or not you generally have trouble remembering material, your ability to retain what you read has probably improved since you started this book. The good reading techniques you learned will help eliminate the major causes of poor memory:

1. *Failure to learn well.* You can remember something only if you first learn it well. The initial impression must be sharp.
2. *Failure to understand.* Confused or uncertain comprehension leaves you nothing definite to remember.
3. *Failure to grasp overall patterns.* Disorganized, unrelated details are difficult to remember. Material is best retained as part of a clearly understood pattern.
4. *Failure to reinforce an initial impression.* An initial impression, whether strong or weak, is retained most successfully when bolstered by subsequent impressions.

As a skillful reader, you have learned how to gain a clear, sharp impression of material, how to understand it thoroughly, and how to grasp its basic patterns. You have also learned to reinforce initial impressions via the multiple readings and recapitulations of the basic reading pattern.

You can further improve your retention by making an effort to *use* what you learn. You often forget simply because you have no need or desire to remember. You should therefore try to develop greater interest in what you learn. Relate it to what you already know. Analyze and evaluate everything you read. Discuss it. Not only will you learn and remember more, but you will enjoy more the whole process of reading, learning, using, and remembering.

Taking Good Notes

A student who studies by passively reading and rereading material often wastes his time. Good studying, like good reading, demands *active participation*. The organizing, selecting, and phrasing of material required in note taking represent the best sort of activity, for each of these steps helps implant the material firmly in your memory. And the notes themselves of course possess great value as a permanent, condensed, and organized version of the original source.

You can gain some of these advantages by marking up the original material. As in note taking, the activity itself aids retention, even if you never look at the markings again. In addition, a skillfully marked book, with key words and phrases underlined, important passages noted, and basic ideas rephrased in the margins, can later be quickly and effectively studied. But this technique has obvious limitations. You can mark up only material that you own, and you will not have the kind of condensed, portable record offered by separate notes.

How to Take Notes

Notes should be easy to take, should accurately reflect the original source, and should be easy to study. You can use the following suggestions to help you work toward these goals:

Simplify your note writing as much as possible by using a system of abbreviations and symbols for common terms. Write mainly in words and phrases, not complete sentences. Your notes should be clear and self-explanatory, but also highly compressed.

Try to reflect the emphasis, organization, and content of the source. Material can be summarized through the inclusion of any or all of the following:

1. Information about the source (title, author, date, etc.)
2. Main idea
3. Important subtopics
4. Details
5. Definitions
6. Illustrations and examples
7. Your own comments, clearly marked as such.

Through the use of headings, indentations, capitalization, underlining, numbering, and similar devices, the physical appearance of the notes can reflect the organization and emphasis of the source. For instance, you can

1. Circle the title, author, and other information about the source
2. Write the main point in capitals, centered over the other notes
3. Underline the important subtopics
4. Indent the details
5. Indicate definitions by an asterisk, etc.

Use whatever system seems best. Standardization of form will make your notes easier to take, more accurate, and simpler to study.

Take notes after you finish reading, with the book closed. Before you can take good notes, you must master the material—or at least learn all you want to learn. Read, learn, recapitulate, and *then* take notes.

Notes taken along the way interrupt the flow of your reading and often interfere with your comprehension. Such notes also tend to be disorganized and indiscriminate, for they are taken before you've gained the overall understanding necessary for intelligent selection. Notes derived from your own recapitulations, however, are usually more condensed, better organized, and more intelligently selected.

Notes should always be taken with the source book *closed*, so that even the phrasing is your own. In every way, then, they represent an *active* effort on your part. Because of this, they will be firmly impressed on your memory.

Take notes that reflect your needs. The *form* of notes, we have said, should be standardized. But the *content* and *emphasis* should vary. You may need only isolated bits of information from one source, and only the main point from another. Occasionally you will want to record even the smallest details. The best notes include everything you need, and nothing you do not need.

Take notes in small batches. How frequently you pause to write notes will depend on your skill as a reader, on the difficulty and importance of the material, and on the kind of notes you want. You can generally take notes whenever you finish a fairly short, unified body of material equivalent in length to an average book chapter. With complex material, you may want to take notes on shorter sections.

Check notes against your source. Before putting your notes aside, check them by skimming quickly through the source, using the techniques of the preliminary survey and making whatever changes or additions are required.

Taking Notes in Class

Some excellent students take voluminous notes in all their classes. Others do well with very few notes or none at all. A good deal depends on your natural abilities. If you have a good auditory memory, you'll find it easy to retain material you've heard. Many persons, though, remember well only after they've seen something in writing.

In either case, your retention of what you hear in class can be improved, just as your reading can, through a more *active* approach. Rather than passively allowing the words to flow by you, keep yourself alert by reacting to what you hear, weighing it, relating it to what you already know, interpreting its significance, questioning it, and challenging it. Even in a large lecture hall where you have no opportunity to speak, you can maintain your alertness by this sort of mental participation.

In deciding whether or not to take notes in class, consider the following questions:

Does the class consist mostly of lectures that present material not available elsewhere? Many instructors do not use a basic textbook. Their lectures are designed to serve as the text, either by covering material not given elsewhere or by providing an overall pattern to which you should relate your outside reading. In a course like this, most students probably should take fairly comprehensive notes.

Do the lectures serve mainly to recapitulate or discuss material given in the textbook? Instructors who use this approach depend heavily on the text to present most of the material, and use class periods primarily to clarify and perhaps expand upon it. Whether or not you need notes depends on how well you are able to read and understand the text, on how much new material the instructor introduces, and on how helpful you find his explanations.

Does the class consist primarily of general discussions? Many instructors expect their students to do most of the actual *learning* from their readings, and devote class periods to general discussions of broad areas, implications, and student reactions to the material. Their aim is to increase your understanding rather than to present new information, and sometimes the nature of the discussion doesn't lend itself to a clear and coherent summary. In these classes, you should probably weigh the potential value of note-taking against the possibility of its interfering with your awareness of the discussion. You may be better off paying close attention and participating yourself, in order to gain the broad understanding the discussion is intended to produce.

If you decide to take notes in a class, they should be designed, like notes from a book, to fit your needs and to reflect the emphasis, organization, and content of the lectures. Accuracy is particularly important, since you cannot easily return to the source to verify them, as you can with your readings. You should also keep them as brief as possible to make sure they don't divert your attention from the lecture.

Since class notes are generally taken as you go along, they frequently give a distorted emphasis to the material. Points that seem minor (or major) at the beginning of the hour may emerge as quite the opposite by the end. It's a good idea, therefore, to check your notes over after class, while the lecture is still fresh in your mind. For important or difficult courses, you may want to rewrite them entirely in light of the overall view you now have of the lecture as a whole. In most cases it is sufficient just to spend a few minutes adding points you may have missed and clarifying the relative importance of various ideas.

Studying Effectively from Your Notes

Basic Study Pattern

The basic study pattern, like the basic reading pattern, allows you to achieve maximum results with material of the greatest difficulty. Since such results are not always required and such material not always encountered, the study pattern should be modified whenever necessary or desirable.

It should also be emphasized that studying is the *last* step in the mastery of written material. It's not concerned so much with learning as with *remembering* and *recalling* what you have previously read, learned, and noted down.

(You can of course study without notes, working directly from source material and using many of the techniques we now discuss. Notes, however, should be used whenever practical.)

The basic study pattern has four steps:

1. Reconstruct
2. Relearn
3. Reproduce
4. Refresh

Reconstruct. No matter how old or faintly remembered your notes are, reconstruct them as completely as you can from memory before you look at them again. This *active* reconstruction shouldn't be omitted, no matter how you modify other steps. It helps reinforce what you remember and indicates—by exposing your weak spots—how much and what kind of studying you must do.

Relearn. Reread your notes rapidly and alertly as often as necessary to relearn them satisfactorily. Concentrate on material you left out of your reconstruction. Skip or skim material you recalled accurately. Test yourself by again reconstructing the notes from memory. If your retention is still incomplete or disorganized, return to your notes. Repeat the cycle of reconstruction and relearning as often as needed.

Reproduce. Rewriting your notes from memory is a highly effective means of remembering material but, because it's also time-consuming, it's usually reserved only for the most difficult or important material.

You can use either of two methods to reproduce your notes:

1. *Boiling down.* Rewrite the notes as completely as possible from memory. Keep rewriting them, always from memory, each time producing a more compressed version, focusing on major ideas. By the third or fourth try, you should have only a concise statement of the main point.
2. *Building up.* Begin by writing the main point from memory. Then add the important subtopics. Continue to add points until you have a virtually complete version of your notes.

In both cases it is obviously more effective to work on relatively unified portions of your notes, covering a single section or topic from the course.

Refresh. As a final step, you should return, if possible, to the *original source material* (not your notes) and survey it rapidly. Even good notes have defects which can often be discovered by a final check against the source. Look in particular for important material omitted from your notes or not clearly explained in them.

General Study Principles

In modifying the basic study plan to your own needs, you should be guided by certain general principles which will encourage you to develop effective study habits.

Set realistic goals—and then meet them. Don't "cram" by trying to study too much too quickly. Estimate the time needed for studying and make sure your schedule provides it. Plan to cover a reasonable amount of work within a specific period of time, and do so. Mild pressure encourages you to work actively and efficiently and discourages daydreaming and procrastination.

Study in spaced periods. If you have two hours to prepare for a test, try to study one hour at a time, spaced at least a day apart. Rather than studying six straight hours the night before an important exam, study one hour a night for the first four nights, and two hours the last night. During long periods of study take short breaks regularly.

Study with a specific purpose. Aimless study is seldom efficient. Work toward a specific objective determined by the sort of knowledge or understanding you want. You should study differently for a detailed command of factual material than you would for a broad understanding of general concepts.

Emphasize what you don't know. Don't keep reviewing material you know well unless you have mastered everything else of equal importance. Your initial reconstruction of notes will point up the areas of weakness that need special attention.

Vary your approach. Do not keep going over material in the same way. Study it from a different angle each time. The basic study pattern automatically teaches you to do this. One time you reconstruct notes, another time relearn them, another time reproduce them, etc. Be certain your modifications of the basic pattern retain this principle of variation in approach.

Seek patterns. Isolated, unrelated details are difficult to recall. Always learn and study material as part of a meaningful pattern. Whenever possible, group material within organized units and clearly relate subordinate details to main ideas.

Use mnemonic devices. A *mnemonic* (pronounced ne-*mon*-ic) device is an artificial but easy-to-remember formula that helps you recall patternless material. The name ROY G. BIV is a familiar mnemonic device which can help you remember the colors of the spectrum—red, orange, yellow, green, blue, indigo, violet. Use mnemonic patterns wherever they can help. Make them up yourself, if necessary. (For instance, you can remember the faulty techniques of persuasion as the "three I's"—irrelevant, incomplete, illogical. Or the basic study pattern as the "four re's"—reconstruct, relearn, reproduce, refresh). Such formulas of course are valuable only in the rote memorization of mechanical details or bare outlines. They seldom contribute much to understanding.

Learn from past experience. Previous exams can be a great help when properly evaluated. You should use them first of all to make a realistic assessment of your strengths and weaknesses. Try to figure out exactly why you lost points on certain questions. Were your answers too vague? Too disorganized? Too short? Too rambling and inconclusive? Did they lack a clear emphasis and correct proportions?

Any time you're not sure why you received a grade, especially if you consider it unsatisfactory, ask your instructor to explain what you did wrong and how you can improve.

Use both your own analysis and the instructor's comments to help eliminate your faults. Some of course may result from poor test taking rather than inadequate studying, and we'll discuss that problem in the next section. But many of your weaknesses probably could be eliminated by more effective studying. If your answers tend to be brief and undeveloped, for instance, make sure your studying produces the kind of detailed knowledge needed to answer questions fully.

Practice under test conditions. You can best prepare for an exam by duplicating test conditions. Most tests do not ask for a generalized summary of everything in the course, and therefore it's usually not very productive to spend all your time reviewing the course from beginning to end. You should instead spend some time practicing what you'll have to do on the exam, namely, answer specific questions within a limited period of time.

Put yourself in the position of the instructor and think up questions that might be on the test. Then try to answer these questions, either in your head or by jotting down the main points you would include. For an important exam you may want to write out full answers under a realistic time limit. Then grade your answers. Check them against your notes and see if you've left anything out. Evaluate your writing for clarity, for concrete details and examples, and for a distinction between major and minor points. Look for ways the answers could be improved.

Many students prepare for tests by working with one or more classmates. After they have completed their individual studying, they join together and take turns asking each other questions likely to appear on the exam. Each then evaluates the other's knowledge and presentation and suggests areas of improvement.

You may be surprised at how accurately you can predict questions, especially if you've paid attention to the instructor's emphasis in the course. You should therefore rarely be surprised by a question on a test. If you've studied efficiently, most of the answers will already have been formulated in your mind.

TEST TAKING

A chemistry test obviously requires different responses than a philosophy exam, and good students adapt their test taking to the particular demands being made on them. There are, nonetheless, some basic principles that will help you perform better on all exams.

No amount of skill in taking tests, however, can make up for poor learning or studying. But this skill *can* assure you of receiving credit for the knowledge and understanding you possess, thereby preventing the common misfortune of doing poorly on a test even though you know the work well.

We'll use as our example a test composed of both short-answer and essay questions. You can of course adapt these suggestions to different formats.

Don't make it difficult for the grader. It's understandable that a student working under pressure isn't too worried about the burdens of the grader. It's hardly in your best interests, however, to make the reading of your paper a chore.

Write in ink, therefore, unless pencil is specifically required. If your handwriting is bad, spread your words out and skip alternate lines, if necessary, to give the grader a better chance of deciphering your answers. Leave wide margins and skip lines between paragraphs. Neatness and legibility aren't merely decorative considerations. You cannot receive credit for what cannot be read.

Survey the exam. Students are often so worried about wasting time that they plunge right into the first question as soon as the exam is passed out. This isn't a good idea. It encourages frantic scurrying rather than an orderly sense of control.

Your first move should be to survey the whole exam quickly but calmly. Find out what is required and what value has been assigned to each part of the test. If there are short-answer questions, see how much they are worth as a group. If the exam is divided into major sections, read the section introductions to learn how many questions you have to answer and how much each is worth.

To make sure you don't overlook anything later on, *underline* the key words in the directions ("Discuss three of the following five statements") and the point total assigned to each question.

Unless there are a great many essay questions, you can skim quickly through them at this point. This will give you a clear idea of what you have to do and will start you thinking about your answers.

Budget your time. Instructors generally indicate the value of each question and the time that should be allotted to it ("twenty points—fifteen minutes"). If only the point total is given, figure out and jot down how much time the question should receive. If there's no indication of relative value for the questions, make a rough guess as to their importance and budget your time accordingly. (You should then make a point, before the next exam, to ask the instructor to include this information.)

Keep an eye on the clock so that you don't spend twenty minutes on one ten-point question and five minutes on another. Even though you're able to write more than time allows, resist the temptation to do so. Select the most important ideas for inclusion and present the best answer you can in the time you have.

Students often claim that a test was "so long I couldn't finish it." This should never happen. Good answers are as long or short as required, according to their proportionate value. By budgeting your time you should be able to finish every test you take. You can do this by making sure that the time spent on each question is commensurate with its importance.

Do the short-answer items first. There's no need to respond to questions in the order in which they appear. The best approach is to begin with the short-answer questions, no matter where they are, since they can be gone through rapidly and don't require planning or organization. Usually you either know the answer or you don't.

If you have no idea of an answer, forget about it and go on. If you have a vague idea, or can limit the possibilities to two choices out of four or five, you may want to guess. If you think you know the answer but can't recall it at the moment, check or circle the question so that you can find it later, and go ahead. You can come back if the answer occurs to you along the way. Try to get credit for what you know without wasting time pondering over or worrying about what you don't know. Go through the short answers at a brisk pace and move on to other sections.

Answer the easiest essay questions first. Again you don't have to follow the order of the questions. When you finish the short answers, glance quickly at the essay questions to decide which seems easiest.

Do these first, since you'll generally be more concise in dealing with material you know well. You'll wander less, bring in less extraneous material, and state the important ideas more directly. Throughout the test, work from the easiest questions to the hardest. This gives you more time to think about the difficult questions and assures you, if time does run out at the end, that your best answers will all have been finished.

Read the questions actively. Students frequently lose credit by misreading questions and failing to write the sort of answers required. Actively seek out and underline the key words in each question. These tell you exactly what the instructor wants:

Define
Illustrate
Compare and contrast
Discuss
Outline
Write fully
List in order of importance
Summarize briefly
Identify
Explain
Comment upon
Analyze

If you're asked to

compare the U.S. Congress and the British Parliament in reference to their authority to levy taxes

do not write a *general* comparison of the two bodies. Limit your answer to the specific topic indicated.

You can also make use of your knowledge of the different types of writing to make sure your answers are appropriate. Determine, for instance, whether you're being asked to write *exposition* or *persuasion*. There's clearly a difference between listing facts and analyzing, evaluating, and interpreting.

It's also important in reading questions to note their various parts and to take care to answer each one:

List in order of importance the basic concepts of behaviorism, compare the contributions of Watson and Skinner, and discuss what you consider to be the chief criticisms of behavioristic theory.

You may want to check off each part of a lengthy question as you answer it. Reread the question when you've finished your answer to make sure you haven't left anything out.

In the same way, you shouldn't proceed from one section of an exam to another until you've checked back to the introduction to make certain you've answered the required number of questions in the section.

Organize your answers. Don't start writing until you've jotted down the main points you want to cover. This lets you organize your thoughts and provides a checklist to refer to as you go along. The longer the answer, the more important this preliminary planning becomes, but it can be helpful even for brief responses.

This rough outline enables you to include all relevant points in your answer, to present them in a logical order, and to emphasize those that are the most important. It also keeps you from wasting time through aimless and disorganized writing.

Stay on the subject. A good answer covers the subject efficiently without a lot of empty words and uncertain groping. The length of your answers should reflect the depth of your knowledge, not a lack of focus or compression.

Eliminate wasted motions. Many students begin by repeating or rephrasing the question. Nothing is gained by this; the instructor knows what he's asked. Nor should you begin with a long introduction or end with a repetitive summary. These are often just skipped over by the grader, who's looking for your *answer,* not for an introduction to it or a recapitulation of it.

Don't try to fake knowledge. Honesty and directness are virtues in any kind of writing, and especially in answering test questions. If you're not sure of something, don't pretend you are. Few students can fake knowledge without tripping themselves up. Answer the question as well as you can, but don't waste your time—and the grader's—by trying to cover up your lack of knowledge with empty verbiage. You'll be better off going on to another question.

Be specific and concrete. Avoid vague generalizations in favor of specific details. Support your statements, and especially your conclusions, with names, dates, and places, and with concrete illustrations and examples:

> Lyndon Johnson's decision not to seek re-election to the Presidency in 1968 was perhaps most strongly influenced by three considerations: Sen. Eugene McCarthy's surprisingly strong showing in the New Hampshire primary, the assumption that Robert Kennedy would enter the race, and Johnson's fears that any hope for a peace settlement in Vietnam would suffer from his involvement in an election campaign.

This sort of detail makes your writing clear and precise and demonstrates a solid command of the subject.

Use lists where appropriate. You can often save time and keep your answers concise by the use of lists. If a number of factual points have to be made as part of your essay answer, it's often effective to use a numbered list. Your overall aim on an exam is to convey information briefly and clearly, and a list can frequently help you do this.

Leave time and space for revision. Form the habit of leaving plenty of space (ten or fifteen blank lines) between essay answers, so you'll have room for additions at the end. You should then try to finish a few minutes early to give yourself a chance to review your work.

First, go back to the short-answer items you checked earlier, to see if the answers come to you now. This can be done quickly.

Then return to the essay answers you feel are your weakest. Reread them quickly and alertly, looking for faults, material left out, and fuzzy passages. Use the space you have left blank between answers to add anything that might improve them.

These few minutes at the end are very valuable. When you read over an answer, you can frequently see weaknesses that you were unaware of while writing it. The addition of one or two sentences clarifying or supporting your main point, for instance, can often make the difference between a bad answer and a good one.

In general, your performance on an exam will depend on how well you've studied for it, how efficiently you use your time, and how effectively you present your answers.

Since your time is limited on a test, the instructor will not expect your answers to be as carefully written as a paper done outside of class. But a good answer possesses the same characteristics as a good essay. It is clear and compressed, unified around a main idea, and well-grounded in concrete examples and illustrations. It is also honest, direct, and free of pretension.

Beyond this, your answer will be judged as a specific response to a particular question. It should present facts when facts are requested, and reasonable, well-supported opinions when such opinions are called for.

Finally, you should remember that, although an exam is obviously designed to test you, it can also serve to teach you. After the test has been graded and returned, you should examine it as carefully as you would a graded essay. Evaluate your performance and make sure you understand the basis for your score. If you're not sure why you lost points on an answer, or how you could have improved your performance, ask the instructor to discuss the paper with you. Find out if your weaknesses were caused by inadequate learning, faulty studying, or some shortcoming in your performance on the test itself, and decide how you can correct these weaknesses. Every test you take, no matter how well or poorly you do, should help you do better on future tests.

Chapter 12

Becoming a Regular Reader

You should now have the potential for becoming a much better reader than you were when you began this book. Only you can make yourself a *good* reader, though, by putting what you have learned into practice, both in school and out.

Reading by Inclination

Samuel Johnson advised that, "A man ought to read just as inclination leads him." Of course, if you read books only as they catch your fancy, you should make sure you come in sufficient contact with books to have your fancy caught. The suggested readings at the end of this chapter can be helpful, as will frequent exposure to the lures of library shelves, bookstores, and displays of paperbound books. You will need little guidance with this approach, for you've chosen a course based on the absence of guidance. All you need is desire and opportunity.

Reading by Plan

A planned reading program lets you organize and integrate your reading for the achievement of long-range goals. Some students, for instance, work toward intensive knowledge of certain fields, periods, or writers. Others strive for diversification. Whatever your plan, make it flexible enough to allow for occasional changes of pace. Many students prefer a combined program—part planned, part free.

Setting Up a Reading Program

Whether you follow a plan or your inclination, decide how many books you will read in the coming year and then read them. A vague desire to read more seldom produces lasting results.

A Minimum Program

Plan to read twelve books in the coming year, or one a month. You should now have (or should soon develop) a base rate of at least 500 WPM. This will let you read and enjoy, and learn a good deal from, a full-sized book of 100,000 words in less than three and a half hours. You can then complete one book a month by reading less than an hour a week.

Many college students elect to read six books a year related to their primary interest, and six clearly apart from it. This helps prepare them professionally while avoiding overspecialization. Even this minimum program can produce impressive results.

If you begin now and stay with it for the next five years, you will have read sixty books—thirty in your field, thirty outside it—in less than an hour a week.

A More Ambitious Program

Avoid an *overly* ambitious program, for failure to meet your goals may cause you to give up trying. If in doubt, begin with the minimum program. But if you're already a fairly regular reader, you can try something more challenging.

At 500 WPM, you can finish a book a week, or fifty-two a year, by reading a half-hour a day. To give yourself some leeway, plan to read thirty-six books a year; that is, three books a month, based on three hours a week of reading. A popular division is one book a month in your field and two outside it. In 5 years you'll have completed 60 books in your field and 120 outside it—by reading only a half-hour a day.

If neither program seems right for you, design your own. But stay with it. A modest program that works is better than a spectacular one that fails.

Carrying Out Your Reading Program

Many students find it helpful to reserve a certain time for reading every day, as part of their regular routine. (Sir William Osler, a famed physician, teacher, and research scientist, read a whole library of books during a very busy lifetime simply by spending the last fifteen minutes of his day, every day, in reading.)

You should read everything—books, magazines, newspapers—rapidly and alertly, varying your rate and your techniques to fit the material and your purpose in reading it.

Make sure you receive a fair return for your efforts; don't plod dutifully through books you find dull. Get what you want or need out of a book. People who feel compelled to study everything frequently end up reading nothing. Read with zest and enjoyment, not guilt-laden drudgery, and feel free to put aside a book that bores you in favor of a more interesting one.

It is a good idea to keep a list of the books you have read, both as a sign of your progress and for the encouragement you can receive from watching it grow.

A Final Word

You can never be a truly good reader until reading becomes exciting and stimulating, for to keep reading you must enjoy it. The skills you've learned in this book are valuable and necessary. But a good reader's blend of an alert mind and an inquiring spirit cannot be gained through technique alone. Without a love of books and a limitless curiosity about life, technical skill can be empty and mechanical.

Reading is not only a supplement to experience; it *is* experience. An author who writes with power, insight, and truth deepens *your* awareness of the world around you and the world inside you. To be deprived of the achievement of great writers is to miss out on an experience that can be gained in no other way.

SUGGESTED READINGS

No sensible person recommends a restaurant or a book without some trepidation. Everyone's taste is unique, and perhaps the best way to introduce a list of suggested readings is to apologize for it. Let is be said, then, that the following selections are no doubt inadequate, lopsided, and marked by serious omissions.

But most students *are* interested in reading and welcome at least some semblance of guidance and encouragement. Consider the following list a place to start, a source of possibilities, an encouragement for browsing. Add to it your own favorites and the choices of your friends. Ask your instructors for further suggestions.

The books have been arranged into general categories for convenience, and brief notes have been provided for nonfiction titles that are not self-explanatory. With a few exceptions, most of the works are from the twentieth century. Some are difficult and challenging, but the majority have proved themselves accessible to intelligent college readers. Some could fairly be considered classics, while others have been included because they're simply fun to read or because they deal interestingly with fields of continuing public interest.

The suggestions within each category are not intended for specialists, but for readers who would like to explore worlds beyond their areas of specialization and who are ready to open themselves to new ideas, challenging attitudes, and fresh experiences.

Ideally these lists could serve—with whatever changes and additions you wish to make—as permanent guides for a long-range reading program which will continue to offer rewards in the years ahead.

The following categories have been used:

Earlier twentieth-century American fiction
Recent American and Canadian fiction
Twentieth-century British fiction
Selections from twentieth-century fiction around the world

Anthologies of contemporary poetry
Guides to reading of poetry
Earlier twentieth-century American and British poets
Some contemporary poets
Twentieth-century drama
Arts, sports, entertainment
Biological sciences
Business and economics
Contemporary affairs and commentary
Government and politics
History and biography
Language
Minority groups
Nature and ecology
Physical sciences
Social sciences
Women

Earlier Twentieth-Century American Fiction

Sherwood Anderson *Winesburg, Ohio*
Pearl Buck *The Good Earth*
Erskine Caldwell *God's Little Acre*
  Tobacco Road
Willa Cather *My Antonia*
  A Lost Lady
Raymond Chandler *The Big Sleep*
Stephen Crane *The Red Badge of Courage*
E. E. Cummings *The Enormous Room*
John Dos Passos *USA* (3 volumes)
  Manhattan Transfer
Theodore Dreiser *An American Tragedy*
  Sister Carrie
James T. Farrell *Studs Lonigan* (3 volumes)
William Faulkner
  The Portable Faulkner, Malcolm Cowley, ed.
  As I Lay Dying
  The Hamlet
Charles G. Finney *The Circus of Dr. Lao*
F. Scott Fitzgerald *The Great Gatsby*
  Tender Is The Night
Dashiell Hammett *The Maltese Falcon*
Ernest Hemingway *A Farewell to Arms*
  The Old Man and the Sea
Ring Lardner *Collected Stories*
Oliver LeFarge *Laughing Boy*
Sinclair Lewis *Babbitt*
  Arrowsmith
Jack London *The Sea Wolf*
William March *Company K*
Horace McCoy *They Shoot Horses, Don't They?*
Henry Miller *The Tropic of Cancer*
Margaret Mitchell *Gone With the Wind*
Vladimir Nabokov *Lolita*
John O'Hara *Appointment in Samarra*
Katherine Anne Porter *Flowering Judas* (stories)
Henry Roth *Call It Sleep*
William Saroyan *The Human Comedy*

John Steinbeck *The Grapes of Wrath*
  East of Eden
Jean Toomer *Cane*
Robert Penn Warren *All the King's Men*
Nathaniel West *Miss Lonelihearts*
  The Day of the Locust
Edith Wharton *The Age of Innocence*
  Ethan Frome
Thornton Wilder *The Bridge of San Luis Rey*
Thomas Wolfe *Look Homeward, Angel*
Richard Wright *Native Son*

Recent American and Canadian Fiction

Tamas Aczel *The Ice Age*
Nelson Algren *The Man with the Golden Arm*
Don Asher *The Piano Sport*
Margaret Atwood *Surfacing*
Louis Auchincloss *The Rector of Justin*
Elliott Baker *A Fine Madness*
James Baldwin *Another Country*
John Barth *The Sot Weed Factor*
Saul Bellow *Henderson the Rain King*
Thomas Berger *Little Big Man*
Ray Bradbury *The Martian Chronicles*
Richard Brautigan *Trout Fishing in America*
Rosellen Brown *Street Games* (stories)
William Burroughs *Naked Lunch*
John Cheever *The Wapshot Scandal*
Richard Condon *The Manchurian Candidate*
Evan S. Connell, Jr. *Mrs. Bridge*
Robert Coover *The Universal Baseball Association, Incorporated, J. Henry Waugh, Prop.*
James G. Cozzens *The Just and the Unjust*
Michael Crichton *The Great Train Robbery*
Robertson Davies *Fifth Business*
James Dickey *Deliverance*
Joan Didion *Play it as it Lays*
E. L. Doctorow *Ragtime*
John P. Donleavy *The Ginger Man*
Ralph Ellison *The Invisible Man*
Frederick Exley *A Fan's Notes*
Frederic Fallon *The White Queen*
Howard Fast *Citizen Tom Paine*
Andrew Fetler *To Byzantium* (stories)
Bruce Jay Friedman *A Mother's Kisses*
Blair Fuller *Zebina's Mountain*
Ernest J. Gaines
  The Autobiography of Miss Jane Pittman
John Gardner *The Sunlight Dialogues*
George Garrett *Death of the Fox*
Robert Gover *One Hundred Dollar Misunderstanding*
A. B. Guthrie, Jr. *The Big Sky*
Oakley Hall *The Downhill Racers*
Mark Harris *Bang the Drum Slowly*
Joseph Heller *Catch-22*
James Leo Herlihy *Midnight Cowboy*
John Hersey *The Wall*
Chester Himes *Cotton Comes to Harlem*
Cecilia Holland *The Death of Attila*
Shirley Jackson *The Lottery* (stories)
Diane Johnson *The Shadow Knows*

Gayl Jones   *Corregidora*
James Jones   *From Here to Eternity*
William Melvin Kelley   *A Different Drummer*
Jack Kerouac   *On the Road*
Ken Kesey   *One Flew over the Cuckoo's Nest*
John O. Killens   *And Then We Heard the Thunder*
Jerzy Kosinski   *The Painted Bird*
Harper Lee   *To Kill a Mockingbird*
Edward Loomis   *End of a War*
Alison Lurie   *The War between the Tates*
Norman Mailer   *The Naked and the Dead*
Bernard Malamud   *Idiots First* (stories)
Peter Mathiessen   *At Play in the Fields of the Lord*
Sara McAuley   *Catch Rides*
Mary McCarthy   *The Group*
Carson McCullers   *The Heart Is a Lonely Hunter*
Ross McDonald   *The Goodbye Look*
Thomas McGuane   *Ninety-Two in the Shade*
Scott Momaday   *House Made of Dawn*
Brian Moore   *The Luck of Ginger Coffey*
Wright Morris   *Ceremony at Lone Tree*
Toni Morrison   *The Bluest Eye*
Alice Munro   *Lives of Girls and Women* (stories)
Jay Neugeboren   *Corky's Brother* (stories)
Joyce Carol Oates   *Expensive People*
Edwin O'Connor   *The Last Hurrah*
Flannery O'Connor
    A Good Man Is Hard to Find (stories)
Tillie Olsen   *Tell Me a Riddle* (stories)
Gail Pass   *Zoe's Book*
John Peter   *Along That Coast*
Harry Mark Petrakis   *A Dream of Kings*
Sylvia Plath   *The Bell Jar*
J. F. Powers   *Prince of Darkness* (stories)
Reynolds Price   *The Surface of Earth*
James Purdy   *Malcolm*
Thomas Pynchon   *The Crying of Lot 49*
Ishmael Reed   *The Free-Lance Pallbearers*
Mordecai Richler
    The Apprenticeship of Duddy Kravitz
Judith Rossner   *Looking for Mr. Goodbar*
Philip Roth   *Goodbye, Columbus*
Thomas Sanchez   *Rabbit Boss*
J. D. Salinger   *The Catcher in the Rye*
Hugh Selby, Jr.   *Last Exit to Brooklyn*
Cynthia Propper Seton   *The Half-Sisters*
Irwin Shaw   *Rich Man, Poor Man*
Wilfrid Sheed   *Office Politics*
Clancy Sigal   *Going Away*
Isaac Bashevis Singer   *Gimpel the Fool* (stories)
Mark Smith   *Death of the Detective*
Steven Philip Smith   *American Boys*
William Gardner Smith   *The Stone Face*
Terry Southern   *Candy*
Robert Stone   *Dog Soldiers*
William Styron   *Lie Down in Darkness*
Ronald Sukenich   *Up*
Harvey Swados   *Standing Fast*
John Updike   *Rabbit, Run*
Leon Uris   *Trinity*
Gore Vidal   *Burr*

Kurt Vonnegut, Jr.   *Slaughterhouse-Five*
Margaret Walker   *Jubilee*
Joseph Wambaugh   *The New Centurions*
Eudora Welty   *Selected Stories*
Jessamyn West   *The Friendly Persuasion*
John A. Williams   *The Man Who Cried I Am*
Robert V. Williams   *Shake This Town*
Calder Willingham   *End as a Man*
William E. Wilson   *Everyman Is My Father*
Herman Wouk   *The Caine Mutiny*
Richard Yates   *Easter Parade*
Sol Yurick   *The Bag*
Lloyd Zimpel   *Meeting the Bear*

Twentieth-Century British Fiction

Richard Adams   *Watership Down*
Kingsley Amis   *Lucky Jim*
Arnold Bennett   *The Old Wives' Tale*
Joyce Cary   *The Horse's Mouth*
Joseph Conrad   *Heart of Darkness*
Lawrence Durrell
    The Alexandria Quartet (4 volumes)
Ford Maddox Ford   *The Good Soldier*
E. M. Forster   *A Passage to India*
John Fowles   *The French Lieutenant's Woman*
John Galsworthy   *The Forsythe Saga*
Graham Greene   *The Power and the Glory*
Aldous Huxley   *Brave New World*
Christopher Isherwood   *The Berlin Stories*
James Joyce   *Portrait of the Artist as a Young Man*
D. H. Lawrence   *Lady Chatterly's Lover*
Doris Lessing   *The Golden Notebook*
Katherine Mansfield   *The Garden Party* (stories)
John Masters   *Bhowani Junction*
W. Somerset Maugham   *Of Human Bondage*
Iris Murdoch   *A Severed Head*
Flann O'Brian   *At-Swim, Two Birds*
Liam O'Flaherty   *The Informer*
George Orwell   *1984*
Alan Paton   *Cry, The Beloved Country*
Alan Sillitoe   *Saturday Night and Sunday Morning*
J. R. R. Tolkien   *The Hobbit*
Evelyn Waugh   *A Handful of Dust*
H. G. Wells   *Tono-Bungay*
Virginia Woolf   *Mrs. Dalloway*

Selections from Twentieth-Century Fiction around the World

Kobo Abe (Japan)   *The Woman in the Dunes*
Chinua Achebe (Nigeria)   *Things Fall Apart*
Jorge Amado (Brazil)   *Gabriela: Clove and Cinnamon*
Machado de Assis (Brazil)   *Epitaph of a Small Winner*
Miguel Angel Asturias (Guatamala)
    El Senor Presidente
Isaac Babel (Russian)   *Collected Stories*
Simone de Beauvoir (France)   *The Mandarins*
Heinrich Boll (Germany)   *Billiards at Half-Past Nine*
Albert Camus (France)   *The Plague*

Louis-Ferdinand Celine (France)
  Journey to the End of the Night
Isak Dinesen (Denmark)   *Seven Gothic Tales*
Romain Gary (France)   *The Roots of Heaven*
N. V. M. Gonzalez (Philippines)
  The Bamboo Dancers
Gunter Grass (Germany)   *The Tin Drum*
Knut Hamsun (Norway)   *The Growth of the Soil*
Herman Hesse (Germany)   *Steppenwolf*
Franz Kafka (Czechoslovakia)
  Metamorphosis (stories)
Nikos Kazantzakis (Greece)   *Zorba the Greek*
Yasunari Kawabata (Japan)   *The Thousand Cranes*
Hans Hellmut Kirst (Germany)
  The Night of the Generals
Arthur Koestler (Hungary)   *Darkness at Noon*
Jakov Lind (Germany)   *Landscape in Concrete*
Andre Malraux (France)   *Man's Fate*
Thomas Mann (Germany)
  The Confessions of Felix Krull, Confidence Man
Gabriel Garcia Marquez (Colombia)
  One Hundred Years of Solitude
Yukio Mishima (Japan)
  The Sailor Who Fell From Grace with the Sea
Alberto Moravia (Italy)   *The Woman of Rome*
R. K. Narayan (India)   *The Vendor of Sweets*
Zoe Oldenbourg (France)   *The Cornerstone*
Boris Pasternak (Russian)   *Dr. Zhivago*
Erich Maria Remarque (Germany)
  All Quiet on the Western Front
Francoise Sagan (France)   *Bonjour, Tristesse*
Jean Paul Sartre (France)   *Nausea*
Andre Schwarz-Bart (France)   *The Last of the Just*
Mikhail Sholokhov (Russia)   *And Quiet Flows the Don*
Ignazio Silone (Italy)   *Bread and Wine*
Georges Simenon (France)   *The Little Saint*
Alexander Solzhenitsyn (Russia)
  One Day in the Life of Ivan Denisovich
Italo Svevo (Italy)   *The Confessions of Zeno*
Amos Tutuola (Nigeria)   *The Palm-Wine Drinkard*
Jakob Wasserman (Germany)   *The World's Illusion*
Patrick White (Australia)   *Voss*
Elie Wiesel (France)   *The Town Beyond the Wall*

Anthologies of Contemporary Poetry

Beowulf to Beatles   David R. Richaske, ed.
The Contemporary American Poets   Mark Strand, ed.
The Contemporary World Poets   Donald Junkins, ed.
A Little Treasury of Modern Poetry
  Oscar Williams, ed.
The New American Poetry, 1945–1960
  Donald M. Allen, ed.

Guides to the Reading of Poetry

Cleanth Brooks and Robert Penn Warren
  Understanding Poetry
John Ciardi   *How Does a Poem Mean?*
Elizabeth Drew   *Poetry: A Modern Guide to Its Understanding and Enjoyment*

Earlier Twentieth-Century American and British Poets

The work of these well-established poets is widely available, either in individual books of poems or in "collected" or "selected" editions.

Conrad Aiken
W. H. Auden
Stephen Vincent Benet
John Berryman
John Betjeman
Elizabeth Bishop
Gwendolyn Brooks
John Ciardi
Hart Crane
E. E. Cummings
Richard Eberhart
T. S. Eliot
Kenneth Fearing
Robert Francis
Robert Frost
Robert Graves
Langston Hughes
Randall Jarrell
Robinson Jeffers
Stanley Kunitz
Vachel Lindsay
Robert Lowell
Archibald MacLeish
Louis MacNeice
John Masefield
Edgar Lee Masters
Marianne Moore
Charles Olson
Kenneth Patchen
Ezra Pound
Edwin Arlington Robinson
Theodore Roethke
Carl Sandburg
Delmore Schwartz
Karl Shapiro
Stephen Spender
Wallace Stevens
Dylan Thomas
Richard Wilbur
William Carlos Williams
William Butler Yeats
Louis Zukofsky

Some Contemporary Poets

Almost all of these poets are represented in numerous anthologies, and in one or more books of their own.

A. R. Ammons
Brother Antoninus
  (William Everson)
John Ashbury
Robert Bagg
Amiri Baraka (Le Roi Jones)
George Barlow
Michael Benedikt
Paul Blackburn
Robert Bly
Richard Brautigan
Lucille Clifton
Cid Corman
Gregory Corso
Robert Creeley
James Dickey
Alan Dugan
Lawrence Ferlinghetti
Donald Finkel
Allen Ginsburg
Darrell Gray
Arthur Gregor
Tomm Gunn
Donald Hall
Anne Halley
Michael S. Harper
Anthony Hecht
David Hilton
Robert Huff
Ted Hughes
Richard Hugo
David Ignatov
Donald Junkins
Donald Justice
Shirley Kaufman
X. J. Kennedy
Galway Kinnell
Carolyn Kizer
Kenneth Koch
Maxine Kumin
Joseph Langland
Philip Larkin
Denise Levertov
Philip Levine
William Meredith
James Merrill
W. S. Merwin
John Montague
Frank O'Hara
Sylvia Plath
Ishmael Reed
J. D. Reed
Adrienne Rich
Muriel Rukeyser
Stephen Sandy
May Sarton
James Schevill
Winfield Townley Scott
Anne Sexton
Charles Simic
Louis Simpson
Robin Skelton
W. D. Snodgrass
William Stafford
Mark Strand
Robert Sward
James Tate
Diane Wakoski
Peter Wild
John Woods
Charles Wright
James Wright

Twentieth-Century Drama

Edward Albee (United States)
  Who's Afraid of Virginia Woolf?
John Arden (Great Britain)

Serjeant Musgrave's Dance
Amiri Baraka (LeRoi Jones) (United States)
   The Baptism and *The Toilet*
Brendan Behan (Ireland)   *The Hostage*
Samuel Beckett (Ireland)   *Waiting for Godot*
Bertolt Brecht (Germany)   *The Threepenny Opera*
                               Mother Courage
                               The Caucasian Chalk Circle
Ed Bullins (United States)   *The Electronic Nigger*
Karel Capek (Czechoslovakia)   *R.U.R.*
Paddy Chayefsky (United States)   *The Tenth Man*
Shelagh Delaney (Ireland)   *A Taste of Honey*
Friedrich Durrematt (Switzerland)   *The Visit*
T. S. Eliot (United States)   *The Cocktail Party*
                       Murder in the Cathedral
Bruce Jay Friedman (United States)   *Steambath*
Christopher Fry (Great Britain)
   The Lady's Not for Burning
Jack Gelber (United States)   *The Connection*
Jean Genet (France)   *The Balcony*
                    The Blacks
Jean Giraudoux (France)   *The Madwoman of Chaillot*
William Hanley (United States)
   Slow Dance on the Killing Ground
Lorraine Hansbury (United States)
   A Raisin in the Sun
Lillian Hellman (United States)   *The Little Foxes*
Rolf Hochhutch (Germany)   *The Deputy*
Israel Horowitz (United States)
   The Indian Wants the Bronx
William Inge (United States)   *Picnic*
Eugene Ionesco (France)   *Rhinoceros*
                      The Lesson
Arthur Kopit (United States)   *Indians*
Federico Garcia Lorca (Spain)   *Blood Wedding*
Archibald MacLeish (United States)   *JB*
Arthur Miller (United States)   *Death of a Salesman*
                        A View from the Bridge
                        The Crucible
Peter Nichols (Great Britain)   *Joe Egg*
Sean O'Casey (Ireland)   *Juno and the Paycock*
                    The Plough and the Stars
Clifford Odets (United States)   *Waiting for Lefty*
Eugene O'Neill (United States)
   Long Day's Journey into Night
   The Iceman Cometh
   Emperor Jones
   Desire under the Elms
John Osborne (Great Britain)   *Look Back in Anger*
                       The Entertainer
Harold Pinter (Great Britain)   *The Caretaker*
                      The Homecoming
Luigi Pirandello (Italy)
   Six Characters in Search of an Author
David Rabe (United States)   *Sticks and Bones*
Elmer Rice (United States)   *The Adding Machine*
William Saroyan (United States)
   The Time of Your Life
Jean Paul Sartre (France)   *No Exit*
James Schevill (United States)   *Lovecraft's Follies*
Peter Shaffer (Great Britain)   *Equus*

George Bernard Shaw (Ireland)   *Saint Joan*
                                   Candida
                                   Pygmalion
                                   Major Barbara
Tom Stoppard (Great Britain)
   Rosencrantz and Guildenstern Are Dead
John M. Synge (Ireland)
   The Playboy of the Western World
   Riders to the Sea
Jean-Claude van Itallie (United States)
   America Hurrah
Arnold Wesker (Great Britain)   *The Kitchen*
Thorton Wilder (United States)   *Our Town*
                            The Skin of Our Teeth
Tennessee Williams (United States)
   A Streetcar Named Desire
   The Glass Menagerie
   Camino Real

Arts, Sports, Entertainment

James Agee   *Agee on Film*
   (One of the early critics of the movies)
Marian Anderson   *My Lord, What a Morning*
   (Autobiography of a famed singer)
Brooks Atkinson   *Broadway*
   (Theater history and comment)
Alfred H. Barr, Jr.   *What Is Modern Painting?*
Leonard Bernstein   *The Joy of Music*
Margaret Bourke-White   *Portrait of Myself*
   (Autobiography of an American photographer)
Jim Bouton   *Ball Four*
   (Candid reporting by a major league baseball player)
Bill Bradley   *Life on the Run*
   (By the Rhodes Scholar who became a basketball star with the New York Knicks)
Harry O. Brunn
   The Story of the Original Dixieland Jazz Band
Jimmy Cagney   *Cagney by Cagney*
   (The career of a Hollywood star)
Marchette Chute   *Shakespeare of London*
   (Entertaining insights into the man and his times)
Kenneth M. Clark   *Looking at Pictures*
   (Introduction to the art of viewing art)
Aaron Copland   *What to Listen for in Music*
Agnes De Mille   *Dance to the Piper*
   (Autobiography of an influential American choreographer)
Duke Ellington   *Music Is My Mistress*
Margot Fonteyn   *Autobiography*
   (Life of a famous ballerina)
William Gibson   *The Sesaw Log*
   (Playwright's report on what lies behind a hit Broadway production)
Richard Griffith   *The Movies*
   (Hollywood history)
Woody Guthrie   *Bound for Glory*
   (An American folksinger's odyssey)
Moss Hart   *Act One*
   (A life in the theatre)
Sterling Hayden   *Wanderer*
   (Self-examination of a former Hollywood actor)

Billie Holliday and William Duffy
  Lady Sings the Blues
Harry Houdini   *Houdini on Magic*
John Houseman   *Run Through*
  (Recollections of a theatrical director, actor and organizer)
Pauline Kael   *I Lost It at the Movies*
  (Notes of a contemporary film critic)
E. J. Kahn, Jr.   *The Boys of Summer*
  (Nostalgic recollections of the old Brookyn Dodgers)
Walter Kerr   *The Silent Clowns*
  (About the silent film comedians, with many illustrations)
Alan Lomax   *Mister Jelly Roll*
  (Study of the early jazz piano man)
Dave Meggyesy   *Out of Their League* ✓
  (An insider's critical look at pro football)
Tom Meschery   *Caught in the Pivot*
  (Woes of a pro basketball coach)
Mezz Mezzrow   *Really the Blues*
  (Early jazzman's recollections)
James A. Michener   *Sports in America*
Arthur Mizener   *The Far Side of Paradise*
  (Biography of jazz-age novelist F. Scott Fitzgerald)
Paul Oliver   *The Meaning of the Blues*
Harold Parrott   *The Lords of Baseball*
  (The men who own the major league teams)
George Plimpton   *Paper Lion*
  (Amusing account of writer's attempt to "make it" as a quarterback with the Detroit Lions)
Ross Russell
  Bird Lives! The High Life and Hard Times of Charlie (Yardbird) Parker
  (Life of a famous jazz musician)
David O. Selznick   *Memo From: David O. Selznick*
  (The golden years of Hollywood, by the producer of *Gone with the Wind* and other movies)
Eileen Southern
  The Music of Black Americans: A History
John Tebbel
  The Media in America: Newspapers, Books, Magazines, Broadcasting: How They Have Shaped Our History and Culture
Toby Thompson
  Positively Main Street: An Unorthodox View of Bob Dylan
David Wolf   *Foul: The Connie Hawkins Story*
  (The realities of life for a pro basketball superstar)
Frank Lloyd Wright   *An Autobiography*
  (America's most famous architect)

Biological Sciences

Isaac Asimov   *The Human Body*
Marson Bates   *Man in Nature*
Jacob Bronowski   *The Ascent of Man*
  (Historical view of the biology and culture of man)
Mordecai L. Gabriel   *Great Experiments in Biology*
Clarence J. Hylander
  Wildlife Community: From the Tundra to the Tropics
William Irvine   *Apes, Angels and Victorians*
  (The impact of Darwin's evolutionary theories upon his times)
Alan Moorehead   *Darwin and the Beagle*
  (Adventures along the way to the theory of evolution)
Samuel Rapport and Helen Wright, eds.
  Great Adventures in Medicine
Berton Roueche
  Eleven Blue Men, and Other Narratives of Medical Detection
John Steinbeck and Edward F. Ricketts   *Sea of Cortez*
  (Gathering marine specimens along Baja California)
Lewis Thomas
  The Lives of a Cell: Notes of a Biology Watcher
  (Witty and provocative observations)
Hans Zinsser   *Rats, Lice and History*
  (Unusual account of the relationship between disease and history)

Business and Economics

Richard Balzer   *Clockwork: Life in and outside an American Factory*
Roger Burlingame   *Henry Ford*
John Chamberlain   *The Enterprising American: A Business History of the United States*
Peter Collier and David Horowitz
  The Rockefellers: An American Dynasty
John K. Galbraith   *The Affluent Society* ✓
  (A study of American prosperity)
  Money: Whence it Came, Where it Went
  (Banks and banking)
Ferdinand Lundberg   *The Rich and the Super Rich*
Sylvia Porter   *Sylvia Porter's Money Book: How to Earn It, Spend It, Save It, Invest It, Borrow It, and Use It to Better Your Life*
William Serrin   *The Company and the Union*
  (Story of the "civilized relationship of the General Motors Corporation and the United Auto Workers")
Alfred P. Sloan   *My Years with General Motors*
  (Autobiography of a former General Motors president)
Adam Smith   *Supermoney*
  The Money Game
  (Wall Street and high finance)
Robert Townsend   *Up the Organization: How to Stop the Organization from Stifling People and Strangling Profits*
  (By the man who lifted Avis out of the doldrums)
William H. Whyte   *The Organization Man*
  (White collar types in big companies)

Contemporary Affairs and Commentary

Saul D. Alinsky   *Rules for Radicals*
  (Advocating community involvement in social change)
Jack Anderson   *The Anderson Papers*
  (The newspaper columnist who specializes in undercover investigations)
C. D. B. Bryan   *Friendly Fire*
  (Death of an American soldier in Vietnam)
Vincent Bugliosi, with Curt Gentry   *Helter Skelter* ✓
  (The Manson murders)

Robert Conot *Rivers of Blood, Years of Darkness*
  (The 1965 riot in Watts)
Fred J. Cook *The FBI Nobody Knows*
  (Critical report on Hoover and the FBI)
Timothy Crouse *The Boys in the Band: Riding with the Campaign Press Corps*
  (Reporters following the candidates)
Peter Davies and the Board of Church and Society of the United Methodist Church
  The Truth about Kent State: A Challenge to the American Conscience
Michael Harrington
  The Other America: Poverty in the US
Eric Hoffer *The True Believer*
  (Waterfront philosopher considers the roots of fanaticism)
Norman Mailer *The Armies of the Night*
  (Protest march against the Vietnam war)
Raymond Mungo *Famous Long Ago: My Life and Hard Times in the Liberation News Service*
  (Underground life in the 1960s)
Theodore Roszak *The Making of the Counter Culture*
  (Influential analysis of the antiestablishment movement of the 1960s)
Studs Terkel *Working*
  (Interviews that reveal feelings of Americans toward their jobs)
Hunter S. Thompson *Fear and Loathing in Las Vegas*
  (Wildly comic view of misadventures in the gambling capital)
James Thurber *Thurber Country*
  Thurber Carnival
  (Collections of witty and humorous essays)
Alvin Toffler *Future Shock*
  (Coping with the world to come)
Joseph Wambaugh *The Onion Field*
  (Realistic account of police work)
E. B. White *One Man's Meat*
  (Shrewd and comic essays)
Don Whitehead *The FBI Story*
Tom Wolfe *Electric Kool-Aid Acid Test*
  (The genesis of the hippie movement)

Government and Politics

William J. Fulbright *The Arrogance of Power*
  (Former senator on the abuse of power in Washington)
Richard N. Goodwin *The American Condition*
  (Historical perspectives on the forces shaping American life)
Daniel Guttman and Barry Willner
  The Shadow Government
  (Influence of private consultants and think tanks on government policy)
David Halberstam *The Best and the Brightest*
  (The Washington brains behind the Vietnam involvement)
Doris Kearns
  Lyndon Johnson and the American Dream
  (A psychological portrait based on personal conversations)
Merle Miller *Plain Speaking: An Oral Biography of Harry S. Truman*
  (Revealing reminiscences)
Donald Riegle, with Trevor Armbrister *O Congress*
  (Personal diary of a Michigan congressman)
Mike Royko *Boss: Richard J. Daley of Chicago*
  (Critical look at a big city mayor)
William Safire *Before the Fall*
  (The Nixon administration before Watergate, by a White House advisor)
Arthur Schlesinger, Jr. *A Thousand Days*
  (The Kennedy presidency, by a historian on the staff)
Theodore H. White *The Making of the President 1960*
  (also 1964, 1968, and 1972) (From the primaries to the elections)
Bob Woodward and Carl Bernstein
  All the President's Men
  (The two reporters who broke Watergate)
  The Final Days
  (Narrative of the end of the Nixon presidency)

History and Biography

Frederick Lewis Allen *Only Yesterday*
  (Popular history of the 1920s in America)
Charles A. Beard *An Economic Interpretation of the Constitution of the United States*
  (The founding fathers as men of property)
James Bishop *The Day Lincoln Was Shot*
  (Hour-by-hour account)
Catherine Drinker Bowen *Miracle at Philadelphia: The Story of the Constitutional Convention, May to September, 1787*
Bruce Catton *The Coming Fury*
  (First part of multivolumed history of the Civil War)
Winston Churchill
  The Second World War
  History of the English Speaking Peoples
    (Both in several volumes; history in the grand manner)
Larry Collins and Dominique Lapierre
  Is Paris Burning?
  (The French capital in World War II)
Frank Conroy *Stop-Time*
  (Autobiography)
Allen Dulles *Great True Spy Stories*
  (By a former CIA chief)
Dwight D. Eisenhower *Crusade in Europe*
  (Supreme commander's World War II memoirs)
Frances Fitzgerald *Fire in the Lake: The Vietnamese and the Americans in Vietnam*
Shelby Foote *The Civil War, A Narrative*
  (3 volumes) (The Civil War, seen from both sides)
C. S. Forester *The Last Nine Days of the Bismarck*
  (Sinking of the German battleship)
Anne Frank *The Diary of a Young Girl*
  (Tragic personal account of Jews hiding from the Nazis)
Antonia Fraser *Mary, Queen of Scots*
R. M. F. Fuller
  The Generalship of Alexander the Great
  Julius Caesar: Man, Soldier, Tyrant

Paul Fussell *The Great War and Modern Memory*
   (The impact of World War I on culture and literature)
Martin Gray *For Those I Loved*
   (By a survivor of the Holocaust)
Lillian Hellman *Scoundrel Time*
   (Personal account of the McCarthy era of the 1950s)
John Hersey *Hiroshima*
   (Report of the A-Bomb and its aftermath)
Paul Horgan *Great River*
   (Story of the Rio Grande)
Bill Hosokawa
   Nisei, The Quiet Americans: The Story of a People
   (The Japanese-Americans)
Irving Howe *World of Our Fathers*
   (Jewish immigrants in America)
James Jones *World War II: A Chronicle of Soldiering*
   (GI's view of the war, with many illustrations)
John F. Kennedy *Profiles in Courage*
   (Stories of Americans who took unpopular stands at crucial moments)
Robert F. Kennedy *Thirteen Days*
   (Inside the White House during the Cuban missile crisis)
Richard Kluger *Simple Justice: The History of Brown v. Board of Education and Black America's Struggle for Equality*
Walter Lord *A Night to Remember*
   (The sinking of the Titanic)
   Day of Infamy (The bombing of Pearl Harbor)
William Manchester *The Death of a President*
   (The assassination of John F. Kennedy)
   The Glory and the Dream
   (Popular history of the United States from the 1930s to the 1970s)
Golda Meir *My Life*
   (The long-time Israeli premier's autobiography)
Alan Moorehead *The Russian Revolution*
George Orwell *Homage to Catalonia*
   (The Spanish Civil War in the 1930s)
Fletcher Pratt *Battles That Changed History*
The Rivers of America (Published by Rinehart, this series includes books on major rivers throughout the country, and on the culture and history surrounding them)
Cornelias Ryan *The Longest Day: June 6, 1944*
   (D-Day invasion of World War II)
Carl Sandburg *Abraham Lincoln: The Prairie Years and the War Years* (Multivolumed biography)
Albert Schweitzer *Out of My Life and Thought*
   (By the renowned medical missionary in Africa)
William L. Shirer *The Rise and Fall of the Third Reich*
   (Hitler's Germany)
Hedrick Smith *The Russians*
W. A. Swanberg *Citizen Hearst*
   (Biography of a newspaper tycoon)
Studs Terkel *Hard Times*
   (Interviews recalling the Great Depression of the 1930s)
Ross Terrill *800,000,000: The Real China*
John Toland *Adolph Hitler*

Barbara Tuchman *The Guns of August*
   (Beginning of World War I)
Barbara Ward *Five Ideas That Changed the World*

Language
Mortimer Adler *How to Read a Book*
Theodore M. Bernstein *Watch Your Language*
   (Practical advice from a *New York Times* editor)
J. L. Dillard *Black English*
Peter Farb
   Word Play: What Happens When People Talk
   (Wide-ranging and entertaining look at the relationship between language and life)
S. I. Hayakawa *Language in Thought and Action*
Charlton Laird *The Miracle of Language*
Eugene Linden *Apes, Men and Language*
H. L. Mencken *The American Language*
   (Classic study of the variety of English that has developed in the United States)
Edwin Newman *Strictly Speaking: Will America be the Death of English?*
   (Television commentator's plea for honest and effective use of the language)
Mario Pei *The Story of Language*

Minority Groups
Maya Angelou *I Know Why the Caged Bird Sings*
   (Personal recollections of black writer and film producer)
James Baldwin *Nobody Knows My Name*
   Notes of a Native Son
   (Black novelist reviews his life in America and Europe)
Dee Brown *Bury My Heart at Wounded Knee*
   (History of the American West from an Indian perspective)
Eldridge Cleaver *Soul on Ice*
   (By a former Black Panther leader)
Vine Deloria, Jr. *Custer Died for Your Sins: An Indian Manifesto*
W. E. B. DuBois *The Souls of Black Folk*
   (Classic by one of the earliest black spokesmen)
Frantz Fanon *The Wretched of the Earth*
   (Influential treatise on the world's "have-nots")
Peter Farb *Man's Rise to Civilization, As Shown by the Indians of North America from Primeval Times to the Coming of the Industrial State*
Harold E. Fey and D'Arcy McNickle *Indians and Other Americans: Two Ways of Life Meet*
Eugene D. Genovese
   Roll, Jordan, Roll: The World the Slaves Made
Dick Gregory *Nigger: An Autobiography*
Alex Haley *Roots*
   (Epic retracing of black ties back to Africa)
Oscar Handlin *The Newcomers: Negroes and Puerto Ricans in a Changing Metropolis*
Langston Hughes *Book of Negro Folklore*
George Jackson *Soledad Brother: The Prison Writings of George Jackson*
   (Bitter essays by the man killed in San Quentin)

James Weldon Johnson
  Autobiography of an Ex-Colored Man
  (Recollections of an early black poet and spokesman)
Martin Luther King   *I Have a Dream*
Oscar Lewis   *La Vida: A Puerto Rican Family in the Culture of Poverty—San Juan and New York*
Malcolm X, with Alex Haley
  The Autobiography of Malcolm X
  (Story of the Black Muslims' slain leader)
Anne Moody   *Coming of Age in Mississippi*
  (Growing up black and female in the South)
Victor G. Nee and Brett de Bary Nee   *Longtime Californ: A Documentary Study of an American Chinatown*
John G. Neihardt   *Black Elk Speaks: The Legendary "Book of Visions" of an American Indian*
  (Poetic and revealing)
Theodore Rosengarten, ed.
  All God's Dangers: The Life of Nate Shaw
  (Oral history of a black sharecropper)
Mari Sandoz   *Cheyenne Autumn*
  (A tribe fights to keep its lands)
Piri Thomas   *Down These Mean Streets*
  (Puerto Rican experience in urban America)
Frederick W. Turner, III
  The Portable North American Indian Reader
Booker T. Washington   *Up from Slavery*
  (Classic autobiography)
Richard Wright   *Black Boy*
  (American novelist's autobiography)

Nature and Ecology

Joy Adamson   *Born Free*
  (Elsa the lioness)
Richard E. Byrd   *Alone*
  (In Antarctica)
Roger A. Caras   *Dangerous to Man: Wild Animals*
Rachel Carson   *Silent Spring*
  (An early call for ecological awareness)
  The Sea Around Us
  The Edge of the Sea
Francis Chichester   *Gypsy Moth Circles the World*
Jacques-Yves Cousteau and Frederick Dumas
  The Silent World
Annie Dillard   *Pilgrim at Tinker Creek*
  (Journal of a year spent observing the cycles of nature)
Gerald Durrell   *A Zoo in My Luggage*
  (Searching for endangered species)
Thor Heyerdahl   *Kon-Tiki*
  (Journey by raft across the Pacific)
Edward Hoagland   *Red Wolves and Black Bears*
    Walking the Dead Diamond River
  (Essays about city and country)
Joseph Wood Krutch   *The Voice of the Desert*
  (Naturalist's survey of unique desert life)
Peter Mathiesen   *Wildlife in America*
Alan Moorehead   *The Blue Nile*
    The White Nile
  (Companion volumes; history and geography of the great river)

Farley Mowat   *Never Cry Wolf*
  (About one of the more misunderstood animals)
Scott Nearing and Helen Nearing
  Living the Good Life
  (Existing outside the money economy on a subsistence farm in Vermont)
Eric Rysbeck   *The High Adventure*
  (Backpacking through the mountains)
Antoine de Saint-Exupery   *Wind, Sand and Stars*
  (Poetry and adventure of flight)
Joshua Slocum   *Sailing Alone around the World*
  (Often called "The *Walden* of the sea")
Stewart L. Udall   *The Quiet Crisis*
  (Thoughts on the environment by a former Secretary of the Interior)
Barbara Ward and René Dubos
  Only One Earth: The Care and Maintenance of a Small Planet

Physical Sciences

Isaac Asimov   *New Intelligent Man's Guide to Science*
Lincoln Barnett   *The Universe and Dr. Einstein*
  (Readable introduction to the scientist and his work)
Stanley A. Blumberg and Gwinn Owens   *Energy and Conflict: The Life and Times of Edward Teller*
  (About the controversial man behind the development of the H-bomb)
Bernard Brodie   *From Crossbow to H-Bomb*
  (History of weaponry)
Lauri Fermi   *Atoms in the Family*
  (By the wife of nuclear pioneer Enrico Fermi)
George Gamov   *One, Two, Three—Infinity*
    Planet Called Earth
    The Birth and Death of the Sun
  (Popular treatment of scientific subjects)
Leslie Groves   *Now It Can Be Told: The Story of the Manhattan Project*
  (The development of the atom bomb)
Lancelot T. Hogben   *Science for the Citizen*
    Mathematics for the Millions
  (Entertaining introduction for the average reader)
Fred Hoyle   *Astronomy*
Bernard Jaffe   *Men of Science in America: The Role of Science in the Growth of Our Country*
Matthew Josephson   *Edison: A Biography*
Thomas Kuhn   *Structure of Scientific Revolutions*
  (Study of how and why science changes)
Hans Selye
  From Dream to Discovery: On Being a Scientist
Harlow Shapley   *The New Treasury of Science*
Wernher Von Braun and F. I. Ordway, III
  The History of Rocketry and Space Travel

Social Sciences

Jane Addams   *Twenty Years at Hull House*
  (Classic account of a settlement house in Chicago at the turn of the century)
James Agee and Walker Evans
  Let Us Now Praise Famous Men
  (Southern sharecroppers in the 1930s; text and photos)

A. Alvarez *The Savage God: A Study of Suicide*
Robert Ardrey *African Genesis*
  (Controversial study of the roots of human attitudes)
M. F. Ashley-Montague
  Man's Most Dangerous Myth: The Fallacy of Race
Ruth Benedict *Anthropologist at Work*
  Patterns of Culture
Franz Boas *The Mind of Primitive Man*
Benjamin A. Botkin
  A Treasury of New England Folklore
  A Treasury of Southern Folklore
  A Treasury of Western Folklore
Norman O. Brown *Life against Death*
  (Speculations on personality, freedom, and inner harmony)
Truman Capote *In Cold Blood*
  (Fictional techniques used to probe an actual murder)
C. W. Ceram *Gods, Graves and Scholars*
  (Exploits of the great archeologists)
George Dennison *The Lives of Children*
  (Story of a "free" school)
Richard Dorson *American Folklore*
Erik Erikson *Gandhi's Truth: On the Origins of Militant Non-Violence*
  (By the noted American psychoanalyst)
Sigmund Freud
  The Collected Writings of Sigmund Freud
  (One of the century's influential thinkers, and a readable expounder of his own theories)
Erich Fromm *The Art of Loving*
John W. Gardner
  Excellence: Can We Be Equal and Excellent Too?
Paul Goodman *Growing Up Absurd*
  (Radical views on American society and institutions)
Harold Greenwald *Great Cases in Psychoanalysis*
  (Pioneering work by Freud, Reik, Adler, etc.)
James Herndon *The Way It Spozed to Be: A Report on the Classroom War behind the Crisis in Our Schools*
John Holt *How Children Fail*
  (Critical view of schools)
Ernest Jones *The Life and Work of Sigmund Freud*
  (3 volumes)
John Keats *The Sheepskin Psychosis*
  (Is a college degree necessary?)
Edward M. Kennedy *In Critical Condition: The Crisis in America's Health Care*
  (Based on extensive hearings before a Senate subcommittee)
Kenneth Koch *Rose, Where Did You Get That Red?: Teaching Great Poetry to Children*
  (A poet's venture into the schools)
Jonathan Kozol *Death at an Early Age: The Destruction of the Hearts and Minds of Negro Children in the Boston Public Schools*
Dorothy Lee *Freedom and Culture*
  (How different cultures see the world through different lenses)
Nathan Leopold *Life Plus 99 Years*
  (Notorious murderer writes with surprising sensitivity of a life in prison)

Richard Lewinsohn *A History of Sexual Customs*
Oscar Lewis *The Children of Sanchez*
  (Life of the poor in Mexico)
Konrad Lorenz *On Aggression*
  (A study of the "killer instinct" in humans and animals)
Margaret Mead *Coming of Age in Samoa*
  (Famous account of first-hand observations)
Karl Menninger *Man against Himself*
  (Exploration of the warring emotions within ourselves)
Thomas Merton *The Seven Storey Mountain*
  (Life in a Trappist monastery)
C. Wright Mills *The Power Elite*
  (The people and organizations that run society)
Jessica Mitford *The American Way of Death*
  (Myth, ritual, and profit that surround dying)
Maria Montessori *The Montessori Method*
  (Theories and practice of an educational pioneer)
Louis Nizer *My Life in Court*
  (Famous criminal lawyer and his famous clients)
Nena O'Neill and George O'Neill
  Open Marriage: A New Life Style for Couples
Robert M. Pirsig *Zen and the Art of Motorcycle Maintenance: An Inquiry into Values*
  (A man seeking sanity; unusual and philosophical)
William Reich *Selected Writings*
  (An influential psychoanalyst)
Jacob A. Reis *How the Other Half Lives*
  (Classic study of poverty at the turn of the century)
David Reisman, Nathan Glazer, and Reuel Denny
  The Lonely Crowd
  (Individualism and group pressures)
Hyman G. Rickover *Education and Freedom*
  (A call for more challenge and achievement in our schools)
B. F. Skinner *About Behaviorism*
  (The leading contemporary behaviorist explains his theories)
Irving Stone *Clarence Darrow for the Defense*
  (Popular biography of the fabled lawyer)
Mark Van Doren *Liberal Education*
  (A plea for the traditional values of higher education)
David S. Viscott *The Making of a Psychiatrist*
Sylvia Ashton Warner *Teacher*
  (Realistic accounts of a teacher's life)
Tom Wicker *A Time to Die*
  (The Attica prison riots)
Edmund Wilson *The Scrolls from the Dead Sea*

Women

Maria Isabel Barreno, Maria Teresa Horta, and Maria Da Costa *The Three Marias: New Portuguese Letters*
  (Their lives, loves, attitudes, and fantasies)
Simone de Beauvois *The Second Sex*
  (French novelist writes a manifesto for contemporary women)
The Boston Women's Health Book Collective
  Our Bodies, Ourselves
  (Illustrated guide for women)

Susan Brownmiller
  Against Our Will: Men, Women and Rape
  (Historical survey and strong opinions)
Kate Chopin *The Awakening*
  (Surprisingly "modern" novel written in the late nineteenth century)
Lee Edwards and Arlyn Diamond
  American Voices, American Women
  (Short fiction by frequently ignored writers)
Betty Friedan *The Feminine Mystique*
  (A starting point for the women's liberation movement)
Germaine Greer *The Female Eunuch*
  (Is society programed for the deprivation of women?)
Karen Horney *Feminine Psychology*
Florence Howe and Ellen Bass
  No More Masks: An Anthology of Poems by Women
R. D. Laing and A. Esterson
  Sanity, Madness and the Family
  (Family burdens and schizophrenia in women)
Anna Lutz *Susan B. Anthony*

Mary McCarthy *Memories of a Catholic Girlhood*
Margaret Mead *Male and Female*
Kate Millett *Sexual Politics*
  (The treatment of women in literature)
Juliet Mitchell *Women's Estate*
  (Marxian analysis of the position of women)
Robin Morgan, ed. *Sisterhood Is Powerful: An Anthology of Writings from the Women's Liberation Movement*
Anais Nin *The Diaries of Anais Nin*
  (In several volumes, by the American literary figure)
Gail Parker, ed. *The Oven Birds*
  (Fiction, poetry, and essays)
Adrienne Rich *Of Woman Born: Motherhood as Experience and Institution*
  (By the well-known contemporary poet)
Wilma G. Rogalin and Arthur R. Pell
  Women's Guide to Management Positions
Betty Roszak and Theodore Roszak *Masculine/Feminine: Readings in Sexual Mythology and the Liberation of Women*